There's No Junior Holy Spirit:

A Supernatural Training Manual for Youth

by Lauren Caldwell

"It makes things easy to understand. It sounds like a teenager wrote it."

Guy, age 10

"God is a really big hero not just for when we die. It totally will help me know how to keep the devil away so I won't be regretting alot when I grow up. Lots of strategies. All my friends should be required to read it."

Ginger, age 12

Thank you Dr. Henry Malone for writing Shadow Boxing©. FMI www.visionlife.org

Collaborator/Editor Kevin McSpadden
Illustrated by Matthew Butcher
Format and Design by Grant Hill

The King James Version of the Bible. ©

All quotations from ESV unless otherwise noted.
The Holy Bible English Standard Version® (ESV®)
Copyright© 2001 Crossway, a publishing ministry of Good News Publishers. Used by permission, all rights reserved.

Kingdom Comics ©

Requests for information should be addressed to:
Garden Publishing Company LLC.
Email:info@gardenpublishingcompany.com
Web site: http://www.gardenpublishingcompany.com

ISBN 978-0-9833377-2-0
Printed in the United States of America.

Table of Contents

Foreword   7

Introduction   11

Chapter One   Gospel of the Kingdom   15

Chapter Two   Holy Spirit Empowerment   33

Chapter Three Healing   43

Chapter Four   Deliverance   53

Chapter Five   Know Your Enemy- Root Spirits   79

Chapter Six   Intimacy with Christ   117

Chapter Seven Seven Spirits of God   125

Chapter Eight Spiritual Gifts   137

Chapter Nine   Five Fold Ministries   147

Chapter Ten   Vision   159

Foreword

I am so delighted and honored to write the forward to Lauren's new release, There is No Junior Holy Spirit : A Supernatural Training Manual for Youth. When I first prayed with Lauren to see her freed and healed from those things that hindered God's love and power in her life, she told God in prayer afterwards that she wanted to do this for others – TO SET THEM FREE!

In order for us to help others be free, we ourselves need freedom. Jesus gave us the power through His name and Holy Spirit, to set the prisoners and captives free from whatever keeps them bound, troubled, tormented, or in shame. Jesus came in love to save us, rescue us, and bring us back home to His Father's home. It all began when 'Heaven invaded Earth!' Jesus came to earth as a man to redeem mankind through His death on a cross, in order to take away their sins, and give them eternal life and life in abundance while still on this earth, with true joy! Love was perfectly demonstrated in all He did, as He went around doing good and healing all who were oppressed by the devil. Jesus saved, healed, delivered, loved unconditionally, and revealed Father God to all who would listen.

The Bible says that "as Jesus is so are we in this world". He is calling for a people who will follow him with all their hearts because they love Him with all their hearts! His love is so great and amazing, that when our hearts have received this love, we are forever transformed and changed into His image and likeness.

Giving your heart to Jesus is allowing God to have full control of your life, and making Him Lord and King. When He comes into the hearts of those who love Him, he begins a beautiful process the Bible calls, "walking out your salvation with fear and trembling".

It is God's design and plan for all believers that they would be free from any lies, torment, trauma, pain, unforgiveness, sickness, demons, or bad thoughts. All believers must be equipped and trained to know their God, and receive power from Holy Spirit to do what Jesus did, SAVE! The gospel of Jesus Christ is very simple, "believe on Him whom He has sent – Jesus Christ", and you will be saved,healed, prospered, made whole, healed and delivered.

The situation for most is, "Ok, I am in the kingdom of God now! I am saved! I get to go to heaven," BUT, they live bound, tormented, sick, oppressed, depressed, and defeated lives! Often, a lack of knowledge or understanding keeps the believer from knowing the full inheritance Jesus died for us to have. Once we are aware of the finished work of the cross, and the power within the believer through the Holy Spirit, we start a journey that leads us to freedom.

This book will reveal to you God's original plan for your lives! Lauren has very simply revealed God's plan to set you free and will ground you in the truth of God's Word, so that you can become a mighty, vicious warrior, and a triumphant, supernatural, child of the living God. It is my prayer that as you read this book, God will reveal His love to you, and that you will be amazed and marvel at how awesome God really is! It is my prayer that as many read this book, both young and old, that you too will say as Lauren did, "I want to do this for others, and set them free!"

Brandy Helton, *President and Founder*
The Garden Apostolic Training Center
San Angelo, TX

Acknowledgements

I've learned these truths at the feet of Father, Jesus, and Holy Spirit, my co-conspirator in love. I am humbled and honored to have been discipled and spurred on by my dear covenant friend, Brandy Helton. I give honor to my amazing husband, Cliff Caldwell, and am more in love with him today than ever before! I thank you Caroline, Guy, and Sophia for sharing your Mommy. Thank you to the faithful, loyal, covenant team at the Garden: Robin, Nancy, Danetta, Dow, Robin, Brint, and Cliff. Thank you to my Garden family, my biological family, and all who have poured their lives into mine.

Introduction

This book is for those of you who know Jesus and have given Him your life. But even if you haven't done that yet, everyone on the planet needs to know about this. If you read this and let Holy Spirit talk to you about it, you will never be the same.

I gave my life to Jesus when I was seven years old. I was in Vacation Bible School (it's like day camp at a church) one summer, and I realized I wasn't going to Heaven when I died. Someone speaking one day at that Vacation Bible School said there were things I had to believe to go to Heaven. One was that Jesus was God's son and that He died to pay for the all wrong things I had ever done. They said that if I gave Him my life, I didn't have to go to Hell when I died. I'd heard about Hell and certainly didn't want to go there. It sounded terrible, full of fire, pain, and fear -- not to mention the devil lived there. But Jesus paid for all the bad things I'd done that kept me from going to Heaven. If I gave Him my life, I would be saved from Hell and invited to be with Jesus forever. It made sense to me, so when they asked, I told someone I wanted to give my life to Jesus. I prayed with them and was "saved."

Shortly after I prayed and gave my life to Jesus, I was baptized. My whole family and I always went to church on Sundays while I was growing up. During those years, I learned to love Jesus and get to know Him as a friend, even though I couldn't see Him. I actually liked to read the Bible and noticed that when I did the things it said, my life was better.

Fast forward about 25 years. Picture me married with two children, still loving Jesus. My husband, children, and I were still involved in church, and we had good friends who read the Bible, actually prayed, and were great Christians. But I just wasn't very happy deep down in my heart. I felt that something was missing from my spiritual life. I had heard stories of miracles, and, every now and then, neat stuff happened in my walk with God, but I knew there had to be more. The problem was I had no idea what that "more" looked like!

Because God loves me so much, He brought me to some friends who did know about the "more," and they began to teach me. An amazing woman of God taught me one-on-one and then wrote curriculum for classes. We now teach most of what I have written in this manual in our School of Ministry. I learned that I have power from Heaven, that Jesus gave me Holy Spirit to help me in every area of my life, and that I had enemies who were trying to steal what God had given me. Most importantly, I began to know Jesus' heart and His plan for my life. I was amazed, and I wished I had learned these things 30 years ago when I first gave my life to Jesus.

I am writing this book because I want you to know this stuff before you are a Christian for 30 years. You don't have to wait until you grow up to be a powerful, loving Christian. Holy Spirit is already grown up. He will lead you. There is no Junior Holy Spirit. I am pretty certain Father God wants you to know this NOW instead of learning it a long time from now. Giving your life to Jesus is so much more than praying, reading the Bible, and trying not to do too many bad things! Read on to find out what I didn't know.

Chapter One:
Gospel of the Kingdom

First things first – what does it even mean to be "saved" or have "salvation?" Here's what I knew growing up: it meant to give your life to Jesus or invite Him into your heart. I didn't have to go to Hell, and I was forgiven for all of the bad stuff I ever did. Not bad, huh? But wait, there's more!

Now you would think if I spent my whole life going to church and reading the Bible, I might look up "salvation" in the dictionary or something. I mean really, if this was for a test in school, it would be a vocabulary word and a no-brainer as a test question! So what is the definition of the word?

When we look up Bible words, we go back to the Greek and Hebrew languages for definitions because those are the languages in which the Bible was written back then. The words still mean the same thing in English, but the older languages sometimes have extra ideas hidden inside them too. It is important to get to the nitty-gritty of the words we look up.

All that to say, if you look up "salvation" in the Greek language, it means:

Sozo /Soteria - Eternal life, forgiveness of sins, healing, rescued from evil, protection, wholeness, and prosperity (to move forward in every area of your life).

So, not only do we get to go to Heaven when we die and get forgiven for all we've ever done wrong, but we also get healed, get rescued from evil, and get to move forward in all areas of our life. We are protected by God as well, and we don't have to have anything missing or broken. Many times in the Bible, the word "saved" could be translated "healed, delivered, etc." Excellent deal, huh? Here are a few questions though…

 Saved from what? Why didn't we just get born this way? Did Jesus really have to die to get something back for us, and if so, how did we lose it in the first place?

Here's a basic version of what happened:

Father, Son, and Holy Spirit have always existed and will always exist. A common question I hear is, "So where did God come from?" Honestly, I don't know. I do know that He exists because the Bible says He does, I see evidence of Him in creation, and I have actually encountered Him in my life. There are people who thrive on a part of Christianity called "Apologetics," (the study and defense of our beliefs) and I encourage you to find out more about Apologetics so you can find specific answers. It would take more writing on that specific topic to explain it, so seek it out yourself.

To continue: Father, Son, and Holy Spirit have always existed. They are perfect in every way. They chose to create a planet with living things on it. I have the idea that they wanted to spread their love, so they agreed together to create a planet and furnish it for their children. The first family was a perfect creation in the image of God. Father, Son, and Holy Spirit delighted in perfect relationship with Adam and Eve.

Some point before time on earth began, Lucifer, whose name means "light bringer," was one of God's angels. The Bible says he used to be beautiful, and his whole body was designed to worship God. Because he thought so much of himself, Lucifer decided he would be the king of heaven and rule it instead of God. One third of the angels joined Lucifer and waged war against God for control of everything. Of course they lost and got thrown out of Heaven by God. We aren't sure exactly when this happened, but we know that it did.

Meanwhile, around this time Father God had created the earth. He breathed life into Adam and created Eve. He put them in a beautiful garden called Eden, and their job was to rule over everything and spread out God's garden across the whole earth. Father God basically gave Adam and Eve the keys to the earth and said, "Let's be a family and take care of this together." I know you are excited about getting keys to a car someday. Can you imagine having the keys to the whole planet?

For a while, Father God and his children enjoyed perfect friendship. God even walked around on earth with them and taught them things Himself. They saw Him with their eyes and were His "BFF's!" They knew what made each other laugh. Father loved watching them learn about and enjoy what He had given them, and Adam and Eve loved their Daddy. It was actually the perfect family.

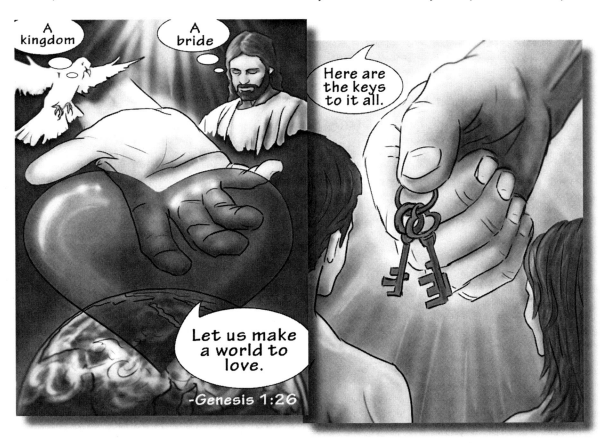

As you well know, every family has rules. This family only had two rules. The first was to be totally obedient to God as they spread the garden, which was a lot like Heaven, over the whole earth. The second was that Adam and Eve were not supposed to eat the fruit of one particular tree because it would kill them if they did. Easy enough, right?

Well, Lucifer (now called Satan, the accuser) hated God for booting him out of Heaven and giving the keys to a mere human. Satan knew he couldn't whip God, so he went for the next best thing – God's family.

Have you ever seen someone rip up a picture or scribble on a picture of someone? It really hurts a person's feelings when someone does that to them. So that's what Satan started doing to God. You see, we are made in God's image. We're like a picture of our Father. Satan tries to rip us up or scribble on our lives because he is no match for the real thing, our maker, Father God. Instead, he picks on us to get to Him.

Remember, Daddy God gave his kiddos the keys to the planet, and Satan lost the battle to rule Heaven. Adam and Eve were supposed to make something like a copy of Heaven on Earth. Satan wanted Heaven, but would settle for the copy. You have to realize that God and Satan aren't equals, so there was no way for Satan to compete with God's power. That's why Satan had to come up with a scheme to gain control of the earth.

Satan knew if he could get Adam and Eve on his side, he could take control of what their Father had given them. It was like a movie where the bitter person tries to steal the family land from those who rightfully own it. Satan fooled Eve. He told her she could be like God and know about good and evil if she only ate fruit from the one tree on the planet Father God said was off limits. Have you ever wanted to do something just because someone told you not to? You've got great-great-grandma Eve to thank for falling on that one.

Well, she listened to Satan and ate the fruit. The sad part of the story is that Adam, who was right beside Eve the whole time, also ate the forbidden fruit. Argh! You may be wondering, "Why'd they have to be such suckers?!" Honestly, they were the perfect examples of what you and I would do, so get over it. But here's where we get into some of the things I didn't know.

Remember, God had told Adam that if he ate of the fruit he would die. Yet, when they both ate it they didn't croak. Say what? Is God a liar? Nope. I'll bet this next part is going to help a few things make more sense for you. It did for me.

God is a three part being in a way. (Don't even ask me to explain how Father God, Jesus, and Holy Spirit are all God, yet somehow separate. They just are. All three are equally God. Yes, even Holy Spirit.) So we are made in three parts, too, according to the Bible. We have a SPIRIT. We have a SOUL. We have a BODY.

> *"Now may the God of peace Himself sanctify you completely, and may your whole spirit and soul and body be kept blameless at the coming of our Lord Jesus Christ. He who calls you is faithful; He will surely do it."*
>
> 1 Thessalonians 5:23-24 ESV

So, how exactly does this work for you? Well first, you have a body, which is made of all the parts of you that you can see and touch. Your soul is your mind, will, and emotions. In other words, your soul is how you think, act, and feel. And your spirit is where your connection with God is.

So what happened to Adam? The best I can explain is that when Adam believed Satan over God and ate the fruit, his spirit died. I always picture it as just going out like a flame. Suddenly, Adam no longer had his connection to Father. That's the bad news. The good news is that Jesus, as the son of God, agreed ahead of time that He would be the hero to come and rescue humanity if they ever needed it. You'll see how that fits soon.

For a long time, I pictured God being really hacked off because of what His children did. I imagined Him kind of turning His back on Adam and Eve and maybe even pouting a bit. Now, I see it so differently. They were God's best friends on the whole earth, yet they believed His enemy more than Him. Wow, poor God's heart. He must have been so sad.

Now God had to get Adam and Eve out of the garden because there was this other tree we don't always think about. It was the tree of eternal life. If they had eaten from that tree they would have lived on earth forever and been separated from Father for the rest of eternity. So He had to get them out and put an intense angel at the gate to keep them from getting back in and getting fooled into eating from that tree, too.

But God knew what to do to make things right, and He already had a plan. Remember, before it all began, Jesus had agreed to make things right for us and be our hero if we needed one. Now, we really needed a hero. So God set His plan in motion and started getting things ready for Jesus to come to our rescue.

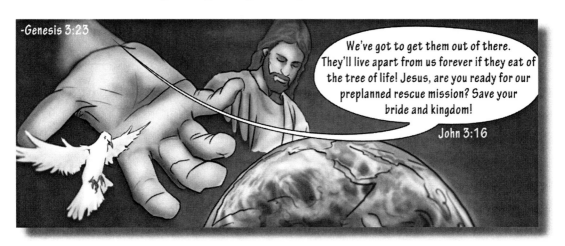

Time out here.

Just so you know, there are some things for which I don't exactly have the answer. Instead of telling you what I think or what I've heard or read, I'm just going to leave it up to you to find out. Maybe you can help me out! For example, you might ask why God didn't zap Lucifer into a Cheeto® and get on with it. I don't know the answer for certain, so I'll let you wrestle that out for yourself.

After a perfect amount of time, Father God worked out His plan. The advertising campaign, also known as prophecies, had been going on for hundreds of years. All the prophets told of a great hero who could come to rescue the world. When the time came, Jesus was born.

Since spiritual death is passed on from parents to their children, Jesus had to have Holy Spirit as His Father. Otherwise he would have inherited His great, great, great, grandfather Adam's dead spirit. And you thought you just got your dad's nose or eyes when you were born! Nope, that spiritual death was passed right on through our ancestors and is still going on with everyone born today. That's why when you were born, guess what? You were not born innocent. Even David from the Bible knew that.

Have you ever seen anyone teach a toddler to be selfish? Nope, we start out with that "instinct." So, that's why when you believe in Jesus and Holy Spirit comes to live inside you, it is called being born again! You are born again in your spirit. But I'm getting ahead of myself.

Jesus was born of the Holy Spirit and a human (Mary) to do what Adam was supposed to do. He's even called the second Adam in the Bible. Jesus was born with his connection to God intact, so He never fell for Satan's lies or temptations. He was the only one who could win the right to take the keys to the planet back from Satan. In order for that to happen, though, somebody had to pay for all the wrong done all the way back to Adam. Jesus had the right to pay for all those mistakes, including ours, because He didn't make any. He perfectly obeyed Father God. Jesus was so obedient that He even obeyed Death.

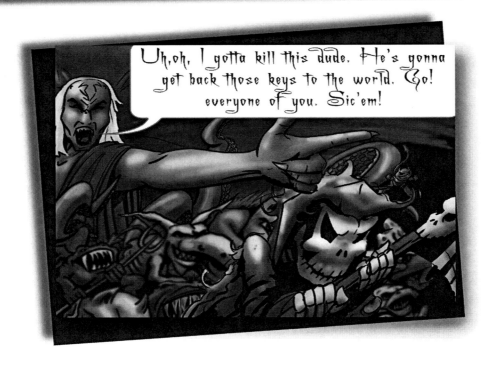

When Jesus obediently went to the cross carrying the entire world's brokenness, Death and Satan thought they'd beaten the second Adam, too. That is, they thought they had defeated Him until God let them know things were good with His family again because the price had been paid. God raised Jesus from the dead to show that all the wrongs were now completely paid for, and we could live again connected to our Father God, just like in the garden.

It is almost like Jesus hit an "overs" button for us all, and we're back to the original plan God had for humans. When we believe Father God loves us and sent His son to pay for our wrongdoings, we gain the advantage over Satan that Adam lost. It's not like God changed His mind about what He wanted to do with the planet! He still wants us to bring His kingdom to the earth. So when we're born again in the spirit, we get to do what Adam and Eve were supposed to do.

Jesus got the keys and authority back and gave them to us. Jesus also gave us His Holy Spirit to live inside of us and empower us to do what He created us to do. We've just got to clean up a few messes Satan makes along the way.

"Whoever makes a practice of sinning is of the devil for the devil has been sinning from the beginning. The reason the Son of God appeared was to destroy the works of the devil."
I John 3:8 ESV

Jesus was punished for our sakes. Satan's power was left nailed to the cross, not Jesus. He disarmed the enemy, made them look bad in public and triumphed over them. The keys and authority are His.

Colossians 2:14-15
Revelation 1:18
Isaiah 53

What's going on in there?

If you haven't come to the time in your life where Jesus Christ has not only saved you, but is your boss, you can do that right now. You can take Father up on His amazing rescue plan. Jesus is the only way to get back what was stolen – your rightful family. If you want to be rescued out of the Kingdom of Darkness and Hell and be born again into the Kingdom of Light and Heaven, today is your day. Pray this or something like it:

"Father , I admit I've done just what Adam and Eve did. I've chosen to listen to the enemy and chosen my own way instead of yours. I was born dead in my spirit and I want to be born again by your Holy Spirit. I want to give you my entire life. I will serve you and love you forever. Please rescue me, forgive me, heal me and bring me peace. I believe Jesus was your son and He died so I didn't have to. Please take care of me and love me forever. Thank you, and I want to have everything you have for me in Jesus' Name."

Now, if you just gave your life to Jesus, find someone else who knows Him and tell them. It is time for you to be taught how this new Kingdom works. Ask your Heavenly Father to help you find someone to grow you up into a mighty vicious warrior for His glory.

Gospel of the Kingdom
vs.
Gospel of Salvation

What is the difference between the Gospel of the Kingdom and the Gospel of Salvation? Once again, let's get definitions of what we're talking about.

Gospel- something regarded as true and believed, good news
Kingdom- where a king or queen rules, a domain
Dominion- a land or territory where a king rules and has authority
Salvation- Sozo /Soteria - forgiveness of sins, eternal life, healing, rescued from evil, protection, wholeness, and provision-(going forward in all areas of your life)

So when we talk about the Gospel of Salvation, we are talking about all of those things described under Salvation happening within us and for us. The Gospel of the Kingdom is basically extending what's happening within us to the territory around us. That's why in Matthew chapter 6 Jesus taught us to pray, "Your kingdom come, Your will be done, on earth as it is in Heaven." We bring one kingdom to take the place of another. We make a transfer from Earth's kingdom to Heaven's Kingdom.

My family lives on a ranch in West Texas. This ranch has been passed down or inherited in this family for five generations. Ranches have boundaries and gates. Entering the gates of the ranch is like receiving salvation. You get in and it is your inheritance. You are happy to be in and receive the benefits, but wouldn't it be silly if you only sat inside the gates? You would miss out on all the fun stuff there is to do and see in the ranch! Plus there's work to do on a ranch. There are things that need to be repaired, pests to run off, and improvements to make. Doing the work on the ranch and maintaining or extending the land are good examples of dominion and a kingdom. Father God is the owner and boss of the ranch and we are co-heirs with Jesus. We do what the Father says in partnership with Jesus. The Holy Spirit gives us instruction and power to take care of the ranch. Or the garden. Or the whole world.

Then Jesus came to them and said, "All authority in heaven and on earth has been given to me. Therefore go and make disciples of all nations, baptizing them in the name of the Father and of the Son and of the Holy Spirit, and teaching them to obey everything I have commanded you. And surely I am with you always, to the very end of the age.

-Matthew 28:18-20

Questions For Chapter One

1.   Sozo/Soteria includes 1) _____ of sins 2) _____ life with God
    3) healing for body and _____ 4) rescue from _____ 5)
    protection 6) wholeness 7) _____.

2.   We are made of three parts: 1)_____ 2) _____3) spirit.

3.   According to 1 John 3:8 the reason the Son of God appeared was
    _____.

4.   The Gospel of Salvation is like _____ the gates of a ranch.

5.   Doing the work or extending the ranch is like the Gospel of the _____.

Chapter Two:
Holy Spirit Empowerment

Guess what? According to Jesus, you are a saint! If you read the beginning of a lot of the books of the New Testament Paul wrote, you'll see he wrote them to the saints. Not sinners, but saints, and that means you. It doesn't mean you should get a statue and people should pray to you. Saint is the name of a citizen of the Kingdom of God. If you are born again, you go from the kingdom of evil to the Kingdom of God, so you are a saint.

How did we get to be so important? Remember that God made the planet because He wanted to love us, so we've just been brought back to where we started. But as you learned in the last chapter, that didn't happen without a cost.

God set the world up to run on unusual types of trade. It's kind of like when you are shopping. You trade money for the T-shirt or CD you want to buy. You have to give the store the amount of money they think the shirt or CD is worth, and that is called trade value. To God, the highest trade value for a life is in blood.

Have you ever seen someone make a deal with someone else and make themselves blood brothers? Or have you ever heard someone say they wanted something signed in blood? These modern examples are a picture of how important and serious it is when you do something with blood. The idea is that something done with blood is extremely difficult to undo. Even the bad guys get this one. Why do you think all those evil things are always so interested in blood? As saints it is important for you to know the power of blood.

Like I said, God set things up so blood holds the highest importance in trade. It is worth more than gold. You can live without gold, but not without blood. You are so important and have such high value that Jesus made the highest possible trade for you. Satan owned your life, but Jesus traded His life for yours. He paid for you with all of His blood, which killed Him, so you now belong to Jesus. That is huge.

When Satan tries to accuse you and make you think He still has a right to your life, you have the right to remind him that Jesus' blood was your price and it has been paid. You have been bought with the blood of God. Wow. So, if accusations come against you or you are tempted to sin, you can say something like, "I'm paid for and covered in the blood of Jesus." And since Jesus' blood is the most powerful trade value, those tempters and accusers have to listen. That's called "authority."

You know how you have to do what your mom and dad tell you to do? Or at school, when the principal says something, have you noticed that people listen up and do what the principal says? That is authority – the power to command something and see that it is obeyed.

Through His blood, Jesus gave his saints the authority to go into the world on His behalf. He taught His disciples (you and I included) that all authority on Heaven and Earth belonged to Him, and He gave it to us. Check out John 20:21 and Matthew 28:18.

> "Jesus said to them again, "Peace be with you. As the Father has sent me, even so I am sending you." And when He had said this, He breathed on them and said to them, "Receive the Holy Spirit. If you forgive the sins of any, they are forgiven them; if you wish to withhold forgiveness from any, it is withheld."   John 20:21-23 ESV

> "And Jesus came and said to them, "All authority in heaven and on earth has been given to Me. Go therefore and make disciples of all nations, baptizing them in the name of the Father and Son and of the Holy Spirit, teaching them to observe all that I have commanded you. And behold, I am with you always, to the end of the age."   Matthew 28:18 ESV

As the Father sent Jesus, He sent us. Because we are bought and cleansed by the blood, we saints are sent out to the places we study, play, and work to make disciples as we go. We don't just go on our own, though. Remember, when we are born again, Jesus' Spirit comes to live inside us and also work in, on, and through us. When we go forth and let Holy Spirit do His work, we are exercising the authority of Jesus.

Another way we show our authority is by using the power of Jesus' name. Imagine two children arguing over something. One runs to the mother to tell on the other. The mom sends back the orders for the fighting to stop. One child tells the other, "Mom said you have to stop." Just like that, the fight is over. Well guess what? We saints are in a fight, too. When the enemy tries to battle with us, we go to Jesus. There is authority in the mom's name when the kid uses it right? Wouldn't you think Jesus' name would carry that much authority and more? So, when we say Jesus' name to the enemy, he knows who has the right to enforce what we say. If he doesn't stop, Jesus will stop him.

When saints speak Jesus' name, Heaven also hears and responds. Father God hears us using His son's name and loves to answer us. Even the angels hear

His name and perk up. They do what God says, and when they hear God's name, they are ready to jump into action.

The blood and the name of Jesus are two basic forms of authority Jesus gives us when we enter His Kingdom. But authority by itself isn't always enough. Somebody has to make sure that people actually do what the authority says. I've heard Kenneth Copeland teach it something like this: Jesus makes us his deputies on earth. The badge He gives us is our authority to enforce the rules of the Kingdom of Heaven. He also gives us the gun for the power.

In the Bible, the word "power" comes from the Greek "dunemas," which means the kind of power released when dynamite explodes. That's a lot of power! We get this dynamite power through Holy Spirit empowerment.

After Father God's resurrection power brought Jesus back to life, He visited His disciples and appeared to people for several days to prove He was alive. The disciples were born again because they believed Jesus was the Son of God, died, and was raised from the dead. Jesus breathed on them, and they received His Spirit. Remember, Father did that with Adam!

Next, Jesus promised his followers He would send His Holy Spirit to give them dynamite power. The disciples obeyed Jesus, and Holy Spirit came upon them in a serious way. Read the book of Acts in the Bible. Before, they had been baptized in water. Now, they were baptized in the fire of Jesus' Spirit. They spoke in new tongues, healed the sick, turned people to Jesus, and basically started changing the earth to look more like the Kingdom of God. How cool is that?

When all that started happening, it fulfilled a promise Jesus had made to the disciples in John 14:12. He told them that those who believed in Him would do even greater things than He did. The best part is that the power was not only for those disciples in that time. It is for you and me today.

To summarize, Jesus paid the highest price for you: His own blood. That blood transferred you into His kingdom. Since you are a citizen of His kingdom, you are a saint who has the right to exercise the authority of Jesus' blood and His mighty name. But you also need power to help you live in that authority. The baptism of the Holy Spirit allows saints to walk in the authority and power of Jesus here on the earth.

As one of Jesus' saints, you get the privilege of taking His love, His authority, and His power to a world that really needs it. Friend, you are like a stick of Jesus dynamite just looking for a chance to explode!

Baptism of the Holy Spirit: My Experience and Yours

"Now John was clothed with camel's hair and wore a leather belt around his waist and ate locusts and wild honey. And he preached, saying, "After me comes he who is mightier than I, the strap of whose sandals I am not worthy to stoop down and untie. I have baptized you with water, but He will baptize you with the Holy Spirit."   Mark 1:6 ESV

I was baptized (dunked on purpose) by a preacher in water to show everyone I was born again into the family of Jesus. But Jesus Himself baptized me in His Spirit! This is for you, too. Jesus told us to be baptized in water and in His Spirit to receive dynamite power. If you haven't done those things, ask Holy Spirit to show you a fellow believer who will baptize you in water, and ask Jesus to baptize you in His Spirit.

Once that has happened, you can do the things Jesus did by the power of His Spirit in and upon you! It is Christ in us that is the hope of glory according to Colossians 1:27.

"To them God chose to make known how great among the Gentiles are the riches of the glory of this mystery, which is Christ in you, the hope of glory."   Colossians 1:27 ESV

I once had a dream in which I jumped into Jesus' mouth headfirst. I was inside Him literally. My head was at His feet – a position of humility. So, when I read "Christ in you," I really think about it!

When the Bible says "Christ in you," that means Jesus is really living in you, changing you to be like Him. We are in Him, like I was in the dream. He is also in us.

Often, when you get baptized in His Spirit (other times too), it changes you so deeply you even get spiritual language downloaded. This is called praying in the Spirit. You just begin to speak out the words that are coming from within you. You may not understand it, and neither may anyone else. That is okay. This is a supernatural way of speaking in the Spirit, so understanding is not necessary. Through this kind of prayer, you communicate with God, strengthen and feed your spirit, give thanks to God, and just enjoy a private conversation with your Father. You may even sing. This is different than when the Spirit speaks through you for other people and it is interpreted. This kind of language is just between you and God, so go for it.

You can pray in the Spirit any time of day doing anything. In fact, the Bible says you should do it always, and it is a weapon against the enemy in the list of the Armor of God in Ephesians 6. Use it!

Questions for Chapter Two

1. _____ has the highest trade value for life.

2. ____ authority on Heaven and Earth was given to _____ first, and then He gave it to_____.

3. We do things Jesus did by the power of His Spirit ___ and _____ you.

4. John baptized with water, and Jesus baptizes with _____ according to Mark 1:6

5. "_____ _____ _____the hope of Glory…" Colossians 1:27

Chapter Three:
Healing

Since He loves us so much and wants to have fun with us, Holy Spirit gives us many gifts. Check out 1 Corinthians chapters 12, 13, and 14. As you can see, Holy Spirit gives many gifts, but the specific gift I'd like to address in this chapter is healing. I won't go into detail and teach all about it because that would be several manuals' worth of material. I just want to help you understand that God is happy about healing, and it is still supposed to happen these days.

I'll tell you this: I've noticed that if someone has a hard time believing healing is God's will, they have a really hard time with all of the other supernatural parts of God. This seems like a bit of a deal-breaker issue when it comes to the supernatural. To put it bluntly, you either believe healing is God's will, or you don't. I recommend you choose to believe in healing right now before you even go on. You are called a "believer" not a "doubter." Besides, the Bible totally supports supernatural healing!

Here's a simple way I understand how Father feels about healing. Remember that healing is a part of salvation/sozo/soteria. The Bible says again and again that it is God's will for everyone to be saved, right? Well, since healing is a part of salvation, God isn't going to take away one of the things Jesus paid for with His blood. Father didn't change His mind about forgiveness of sins or eternal life. He hasn't changed His mind about healing either.

I know people sometimes ask, "Well, what about when people aren't healed? Does that mean it is God's will for them to be sick?" I'll answer a question with a question: "Well, what about people who go to hell or aren't born again? Was that God's will?" Heck, no! God wants every single person to be with Him.

I'll be honest. I don't know why some people are healed and others aren't. I don't know why some people believe Jesus while others aren't saved. I do know the enemy has a hand in whether someone is healed, as well as the way people respond to the Gospel. Satan's job is to steal, kill, and destroy. He is always trying to do those things to people, but that doesn't mean it is God's will or that He wants that to happen.

At one time, I believed God made people sick to teach them a lesson. I know that sounds totally opposite from everything else I've taught you about Father. Well, that's because thinking God does that to people is wrong.

Wouldn't you think I was a sick-o if I gave my baby a disease to teach her to obey me? How about if I broke my son's arm to teach him patience? Crazy, I know.

Yes, God can teach me anything, any time, and anywhere. But He doesn't have to be a sick-o to do it. God's got a million other cool ways to teach me what He wants me to learn. If you've believed that God has hurt you to teach you things, just tell Him you're sorry and ask Him to forgive you for believing such junk.

God did not create people to live in sin, sickness, or disease. Just read the Gospels and look at what Jesus did when people were hurt or sick.

Jesus told the disciples if they'd seen Him they'd seen the Father. Jesus also said He only did what He saw His Father doing and said what He heard Him saying. So, Jesus is the perfect picture of God's will. One man even asked Jesus if He was willing to heal him. Jesus said He was willing. There ya go. Jesus said it. There's a real clear answer about God's will to heal.

> *"And behold, a leper came to him and knelt before Him, saying, 'Lord, if you will, you can make me clean.'"And Jesus stretched out His hand and touched him, saying, 'I will; be clean.' And immediately his leprosy was cleansed."*   Matthew 8:2, 3 ESV

Again and again Jesus knocked sickness off people and healed their hurts. Yet, others still suffered from pain and disease. How did this happen? God isn't confused about His desire to heal people. God is always good and perfect, so it's obvious the problem isn't on His end. It must be coming from somewhere else.

Often times there are some spiritual causes behind sickness and pain. Sometimes a demon or evil spirit is what makes the person sick. If we want to overcome these spirits and see people freed and healed, we have to stay close to Jesus to hear what He wants us to do. He has already beaten those spirits and diseases, and He will surely lead us in victory.

You may wonder what to do when you believe with all your heart, pray as hard as you can, and do everything you know to do, but someone still doesn't get healed. I realize there's a lot we don't know about healing, but I do know Jesus told us to go out and heal people, teach others about Him, use His power to defeat Satan, and bring the lost back to His love. Yes, it hurts when what I pray doesn't show up on earth. Yes, I get bummed and sometimes want to quit. But

Jesus was hurt and tempted to quit, too. Yet He kept on going for my sake, so I will keep going for Him.

We are believers, so we keep on believing, no matter what!

So how do you pray for people to be healed? There is no certain way to do it every time, but here's an example you can follow. This is based upon the 5-step Prayer Model for Healing and 10-step Model for Deliverance from Global Awakening. The important thing, however, is to listen to Holy Spirit and do whatever He tells you.

1. Ask Questions to find out the root cause of the problem.

It is often one of the following: an evil spirit, a curse, something from their soul/mind, or natural causes like accident, injury, or disease. If you figure out there are a lot of heavy demonic things to deal with and they aren't believers, lead them first to Jesus before going through deliverance (casting out demons). If they refuse Jesus strongly, it is a good idea to bless them and go on. You must follow Holy Spirit on this one.

1) What is your name?
2) How can I pray for you?
3) How long has this been a problem?
4) How or when did it start?
5) Why do you think you have this problem?
6) Did someone cause this? Have you forgiven them?
7) Did something bad happen around the time this began?

Basic Prayer Choices

1. Request- "Father, in Jesus' name, I ask you to heal the redness in Jane's knee and take away the swelling and pain."

2. Command- "In the name of Jesus, I command the redness in Jane's knee to be healed and all the swelling and pain to leave."

  a. Use commands when destroying a curse or vow, casting out a spirit, when you've used request prayers and the healing has stopped, or whenever Holy Spirit tells you to.

2. Tips for praying

a. Ask Holy Spirit to be there with His guidance and healing power.
b. Ask the person to be quiet and just focus on their body and receive.
c. Ask them to tell you if anything starts happening. Many people feel warmth.
d. Keep your eyes open, you can often see what's happening.
e. Have the person confess sin or close doors in the spirit (more about that later) before you pray for healing in their body.
f. Always pray in Jesus' name.
g. Don't pray or talk a long time if nothing's happening.
h. If something's working, keep on doing it.
i. Pray about what's making them feel bad and what they feel.
j. Trust Holy Spirit.
k. Thank God all the Time!

3. Stop and ask more questions

a. Has the pain moved or changed? If the pain moves, it's almost always a spirit.
b. Has anyone in your family dealt with this too?
c. Is there anything you are really afraid of?
d. Has anyone ever spoken a curse over you? Have you said anything bad about yourself?
e. Has anyone or is anyone in your family messing with satanic stuff or a member of the freemasons?
f. Do you have accidents often? If so, find the open door to a deaf and dumb spirit, close it, and command it to leave.

4. Stop praying for healing when they are healed, you feel Holy Spirit tell you to stop, or you are not making any progress at all.

5. When you finish…

a. Encourage them with what you know from the Bible or what some one else has taught you that's helped you.
b. Share with them things they might do to change the lifestyle that got them there to begin with…do not get preachy!

c. NEVER blame the person if they do not get healed. Encourage and bless them in every way and offer to pray for them again some other time.

d. If they don't know Jesus as Savior and Lord, invite them to give their lives to Him. Doesn't have to be fancy, just share what you know about the Gospel of the Kingdom and invite them in. They can pray after you something like:

"Jesus , I know I am not in your Kingdom because of what I've done. Please take my whole life and do with it as you wish. I believe You are God's Son and You died for my punishment. Please forgive me and give me Your Spirit inside and baptize me in Your Spirit for empowerment. I want total healing for my body and soul, peace and rescue from evil. Please take care of me and provide for me. I receive it in Jesus' name. Amen."

e. If they know someone's been praying for them, have them contact that person and tell them what's happened in their lives.

f. Get their info and call them in a day or two. Give them your info and you just might be making a disciple. Don't harass them, just follow Holy Spirit.

Make a copy of these pages and take them with you wherever you go!

Questions for Chapter Three

1.   Gifts of Holy Spirit are listed in 1 Corinthians_____.

2.   Healing is part of salvation. T/F

3.   Father created people to live in sin, sickness and disease. T/F

4.   A demon is never to blame when someone is sick. T/F

5.   Two basic types of prayers in healing are_____ and _____.

Chapter Four:
Deliverance

Remember how I mentioned that evil spirits or demons might have something to do with sin, sickness or disease? Let's look a bit deeper into that.

If God had a closet, it would look way better than yours. Everything would be picked up and put in its place. If He had a locker, it would be perfectly organized. He would know right where all His things were at all times. You see, God is extremely organized because He loves order. His order may look messy from our point of view, but He has a much better view from where He is. It is our choice to trust Him and follow His order.

I've provided an illustration of God's order a little later in this chapter. For now, just understand that God has set things up a certain way for a reason.

The problem is that Satan has tried to make a complicated mess out of God's intended order. One of the best ways he's managed to do that is to keep humans confused about who we really are. He sometimes tricks us into forgetting about our connection with Father and our privileges as His children, so we may not live out all that God has planned for us. Fortunately, Holy Spirit helps believers overcome the devil's tricks.

God's saints need to remember that Jesus made a way for us to come back to what Father had planned for us all along. In Psalm 8, the Bible says we were created just lower than God, but above other things. That passage shows how God has put us in important positions and given us authority and responsibility just like He did Adam and Eve.

Those verses in Psalm 8 also mention angels, so I want to discuss them here. First, we never worship angels. A few folks in the Bible tried to worship them, and the angels responded by being horrified that people would do such a thing! God's angels direct all attention to our Father, and they refuse to accept worship, which only belongs to Him. If an angel ever accepts worship, that's a big hint it belongs to Satan's team.

Second, Father has chosen angels to help us bring His Kingdom to earth. As the verses below prove, angels listen for us to speak God's word so they can perform it, or carry out what it says. Though we do not worship them, we are very grateful that God uses them to help us.

Finally, when you die, you will not turn into an angel. That is an idea many people believe, but it is definitely not in the Bible.

"Are they not all ministering spirits, sent out to serve for the sake of those who are to inherit salvation?"   Hebrews 1:14 ESV

"Do you not know that we are to judge angels? How much more, then, matters pertaining to this life?"   1 Corinthians 6:3 ESV

"Bless the LORD, O you His angels, you mighty ones who do His word, obeying the voice of His word! Bless the Lord all His hosts, His ministers, who do His will! Bless the Lord, all His works, in all places of his dominion. Bless the LORD, O my soul!"   Psalm 103:20-22 ESV

These verses prove that angels are actively involved in our lives. The verse from 1 Corinthians even says we will judge them. To judge means to decide how well someone has carried out a law or command. How can we judge angels if we never utilize them? Let me be clear. We do not pray to angels. We release Father's word as He puts it in our hearts, and they do what He says through us. It doesn't necessarily mean we have to quote Scripture. It means what we say must line up or agree with God's will. When our words match up with God's will, the angels act on what we say.

Many times you will be aware that angels are present. You just kind of know they are with you. You may even see angels with your eyes. I have seen one angel with my open eyes. As you can expect from reports in Scripture, I was scared. I literally hid under my covers until it left. Wish I could redo that opportunity. So learn from my mistake and don't be surprised at the realm of the supernatural showing up when you begin to live more aware of spiritual reality. I've "seen" other angels more in my mind's eye (that part of your mind where you imagine things). I have also had the impression (strong feeling) they were around me tons of times. So, just like in the Bible, ask God to open your eyes to see what's really there.

Okay, so we know that angels and evil spirits are real. We know that God the Father, Son, and Holy Spirit rule over everything, and we know that people have an important place in it all. So how does this all fit together? That is where God's order comes into play.

"For by Him all things were created, in heaven and on earth, visible and invisible, whether thrones or dominions or rulers or authorities-all things were created through him and for him."   Colossians 1:16 ESV

God's Hierarchy of Authority

God the Father

God the Son

God the Holy Spirit

Redeemed Man

Holy Beings (Angels) in Ranking Order

Satan

Satan's Fallen Angels in Ranking Order

Demon Spirits in Ranking Order

Fallen Man

Hierarchy based on revelation of **Ken Howerton** of *Radah Ministries*

According to the diagram, we have more authority than everything in the kingdom of evil. If this is true (and it is), then why are believers getting beaten up by the other side? It goes back to what I said about Satan messing with God's order.

You see, Satan only has a few schemes, but he can arrange them a million different ways. Two tools for his schemes are deception and magnification. He will lie to you about something and then make it seem bigger than it is. For example, have you ever lied about something? Sure you have. When you lied, you fell for a temptation born from the ugliness in your heart, as the book of James points out.

> "Let no one say when he is tempted, "I am being tempted by God," for God can not be tempted with evil, and He himself tempts no one. But each person is tempted when he is lured and enticed by his own desire. Then desire when it has conceived gives birth to sin, and sin when it is fully grown brings forth death. Do not be deceived my dear brothers."
> James 1:13-16 ESV

Satan tries to make certain situations seem so huge that you can't see any way out of them. In these cases, telling the truth and changing your ways seems impossible. You may worry that making things right will result in disaster. But your spirit knows the lie is wrong, and Holy Spirit whispers that you need to tell the truth. Finally, you give in to Holy Spirit and confess the lie. There might be consequences, but most of the time they are nowhere near as awful or big as Satan portrays them to be. He just wanted to make it seem that way to ruin your peace.

If we remember we are saints bought with the highest price, we are much less likely to fall for the devil's schemes. But if we are who Father says we are and have the power, authority, and gifts Jesus and His Spirit give, why do we still seem to get beaten up so much?

I'd like to equip you with an explanation based on the book Shadowboxing by Dr. Henry Malone, as well as other books I've read, things I've been taught, and experiences I've had.

There are basically two methods of attack Satan and his demons use to get at you. One is "intrusion." Intrusion means the enemy blindsides you with all his junk. The other is "legal ground," which you can think of as an open door in your life that gives the enemy access to you.

Both intrusion and open doors stink, but you have been given the authority and power to call on Father for help. You need to be rescued and delivered out of these situations like Jerry getting rescued from Tom in the cartoons. Guess that makes God the lady housekeeper and the angels the broom! Let's look at each type of attack

Intrusion

Intruder Alert! Intruder Alert! Intrusion is when Satan just barges into your life though you haven't done a thing to deserve it. He has no right to be there. Imagine your room as a picture of who you are. Sometimes Satan just busts into your life like a little sister with a handful of crayons. She gets into your space and messes things up. But because she had no authority or right to come into your room and start coloring on everything, you can get your parents to help you make her leave.

When Satan intrudes into your life and you recognize what's going on, you just run straight to Father and tell on him. Since the devil had no right to do what he was doing, God will help you kick that sucker out of your life!

Legal ground

This is when you, or someone in authority over you, has given the authority Jesus gave you back to Satan. This is like you inviting one of your friends into your room even though your parents told you not to. He begins tearing things up and spilling his soda all over your new gadgets. This time, you have to confess what you did and agree with your parents that you were wrong in order to get them to help you kick your "friend" out. Plus, you have to keep the door closed if you don't want that dude coming back!

There are five main open doors through which evil spirits have access to your life. These doors are disobedience, unforgiveness, emotional trauma, inner vows and judgments, and curses. If one or all of these doors is open, guess who has access to your life?

So let's learn what the doors are and how to close them.

Door 1: **Disobedience**

To understand disobedience better, let's define a churchy word – "sin."

Sin - in Bible language, sin is when an arrow is shot and it misses the mark or target. So, when we miss the target Father set for us, it is called sin. Don't get me wrong, Father gives the empowerment and ability to hit the target. However, when we don't know about the target or use the ability to hit it, we sin.

Disobedience - is when we sin on purpose. It's any action or attitude that the Bible tells you not to do or have, but you do or have it anyway. It is also anything the Bible tells you to do and you don't do it.

Disobedience includes some obvious things like getting drunk, stealing, lying, and cursing. But your attitudes, your heart, and your mind matter too. Disobedience starts small but grows. It follows a simple but deadly process: Fascinate, Meditate, Participate. Once you start thinking about sin, you can't stop yourself from sinning easily. The more you sin, the more you become sin's slave. It is like you are bound or chained to it. That's called bondage. Sin will always take you further than you wanted to go and keep you longer than you wanted to stay. Do not mess around with willful sin.

You may have so many sinful attitudes or actions that you barely notice them and they seem natural to you. But you don't get to be the judge of what is okay – God does! If you have willingly been disobedient to God, it is essential for you to repent.

Repent - this word means you are headed one direction, but you stop and go in the opposite way from where you were going. It also means you allow God to change how you think about the situation.

Repenting is not saying, "I'm sorry I got caught. I'll try to change." It is when you see how good Father God is, remember what Jesus did so you could be saved/sozo-ed, and recognize how much you were turning your back on what they did. These things happen in your heart, not your head alone. You know repentance is real when what you do afterward is different than what you did before. Repentance is real if God tells you to go correct what you did wrong, and you rush out to do it. Correcting wrongs may sometimes include going to someone, telling them you are sorry for what you did, and asking them to forgive you. It takes guts to do this, but it knocks the snot out of the enemy!

In addition to asking for forgiveness, you may also need to renounce some o your ways of thinking.

Renounce - to renounce something means you come out of agreemen with an action or way of thinking. It is like divorcing yourself from something or dropping someone's hand you were holding. You no longer have contact with it, and you consider it dead. You say, "I thought this was true or good, but now I know it is not."

So the open door of disobedience means you willingly held bad attitudes or did wrong things. To shut this door, you must repent of your sin and renounce it. Here's an example prayer you can use or fit to how you want to say it:

"Father, in Jesus' name, I agree with you that it was wrong to think about or imagine _____. I am sorry I (insert what you did here)_____ _____. It is sin, and there is no excuse. It was my fault. Please forgive me and cleanse me. I renounce my participation with the sin and any evil spirit connected to it. Every evil spirit must leave me now. Holy Spirit, blow like a whirlwind through me and clean me out. Holy Spirit, fill me up where anything but You took up space, in Jesus' name."

Door 2: Unforgiveness

Jesus once told a parable that shows us what unforgiveness looks like. In that parable, a master decided not to make his servant pay back a huge amount of money the servant owed. However, the servant refused to do the same thing for his fellow servants.

"Then his master summoned him and said to him, 'You wicked servant! I forgave you all that debt because you pleaded with me. And should not you have had mercy on your fellow servant, as I had mercy on you?' And in anger his master delivered him to the jailers, until he should pay all his debt. So also my heavenly Father will do to every one of you, if you do not forgive your brother from your heart." Matthew 18:32-35 ESV

Unforgiveness - is refusing to let go of or excuse a debt owed by another person. It has been compared to drinking poison and hoping the other person suffers. Silly, huh?

Growing up, I heard that we should forgive people, but I didn't really know how. Forgiveness isn't just stuffing something down inside ourselves and trying to forget about it. Stuffing things down is like trying to hold several beach balls underwater - it takes a lot of time, energy, and focus to keep them under the surface. Trying to ignore things doesn't solve the problem; it just wears you out. One the other hand, forgiveness takes all that pressure off of you. Forgiveness is allowing Holy Spirit to pop those beach balls up so He can get rid of them for you.

Another picture of forgiving versus not forgiving is when you get a splinter in your hand. Remember when you were little and your parents had to chase you around the house and hold you down to get a splinter out? Well imagine that a splinter represents when someone hurts you. Father wants to pull it out, but you want to run.

What happens when you don't get a splinter out? Your hand gets red and infected. Imagine evil spirits and the demonic as germs. As long as you're wounded, they can grow and multiply. Eventually, a thick skin grows over where the splinter was. You begin to lose feeling in that part of your skin. Because you lose feeling, you are more likely to get another splinter. Wow. It becomes even more painful, and you aren't about to let Father touch it. The same thing continues until your whole hand becomes sore, infected, and unable to feel much other than the pain.

Now imagine that your heart is like your hand. The more painful things you go through, the harder your heart gets. Suppose one day you want to get all the pain out. Father is still willing to remove all of the "splinters," but it might hurt to go digging around in there amongst all the other splinters. The good news is that if you can stick it out and let Him do what He wants, it will be healed.

So, do you want to know how to forgive now? I thought so. There is not a specific way you have to do it, but there are some things that it really helps to know.

Forgiving doesn't mean what happened is ok. It means you aren't the one responsible for seeing that things are made right. Father God says it's His job to repay and make things right, and you sure don't want to try and do His job.

When you are praying to forgive someone, you will want to pray out loud. Not only does it help you keep track of what you are doing, but the enemy can also hear you, and the demons know for sure they are getting the door slammed in their face. It's also good to have another person there with you. You aren't praying to the person, but they can help you stay focused and listen for other stuff you might need to pray about.

It is also important for you to be specific about how whatever happened made you feel. Emotions and feelings can be healed too. Have you ever heard someone say their feelings got hurt? If feelings can be hurt, then Jesus wants to heal them. Crying is often a great way to get emotions healed. Don't hold it in. Laughter is healing too, so let 'er rip!

When you forgive someone, don't say, "Jesus, help me forgive Jennifer." Jesus already died to give you the supernatural power to forgive. Forgiveness is your choice. You decide in your heart to let it go and you just do it.

Sometimes after you forgive you still feel some pain. Remember the splinter-in-the-hand example? Even after you get the splinter out, it sometimes takes a while for full healing to happen. Getting the evil spirit out helps too, but we'll get to that in a bit!

If you are having a hard time deciding why you should forgive, check out the story Jesus tells in Matthew 18. The parable points out how much we've been forgiven and how it is only right to forgive others. Compare one thing or even several things they have done to you with every sin for which you've ever been forgiven. This helps you see things how Father does.

A friend of mine, Blenda, compares every bit of unforgiveness to a rock in a backpack you carry around everywhere you go. As you forgive, your load gets lighter. Whatever it takes, just do it. This is one of the biggies most people miss their whole lives. If you can catch on to forgiveness, it will forever change your life.

Here's an example prayer you can use to forgive someone:

"Father God, in the name of Jesus, it is my will and I choose to forgive (insert name here) _____ for (insert what happened or what they said) _____. (If it is something they said, you should destroy the power of the words they said and command any spirit assigned to fulfill those words to leave you alone.) When they did what they did it made me feel (sad, hurt, angry etc.)_____. I ask you to heal my emotions too, in Jesus' name."

Door 3: Emotional Trauma

Trauma is anything that causes pain. Hospitals have trauma units to treat people who are in severe pain in their bodies. As I mentioned before, our emotions can also be hurt.

Emotional traumas are inner hurts that can be caused by sudden physical injury or emotional shock. There are two types: traumas we cause through disobedience (which means we must face the consequences of our actions) and those we had no part in causing. Sometimes other people may hurt us or accidents may happen, and those things can cause emotional trauma.

However, there is good news. Jesus came to heal us of both types of trauma. In Luke 4 the Bible tells us that He came to set captives free as well as prisoners. Captives are minding their own business and get kidnapped. Prisoners did something bad and deserve to be locked up and punished. Either way, Jesus wants them free. Remember, Jesus came to be our hero and to rescue us even though we didn't deserve it. That includes saving us from trauma.

"The Spirit of the Lord is upon me, because he has anointed me to proclaim good news to the poor. He has sent me to proclaim liberty to the captives and recovering of sight to the blind, to set at liberty those who are oppressed, to proclaim the year of the Lord's favor."
                                                            Luke 4:18 ESV

When talking about trauma, it is important to realize people are different. Something might cause trauma in you, but not your brother, sister, or friend. For example, your heart may be trashed because your grandpa died, but your brother was only sad for a little while. While it is understandable that you want to be like everyone else and fit in, it is also true that there is no one else like you on the planet.

Here is one way of understanding how trauma works: What happens when you are shocked or scared? You suck in air through your mouth. Imagine that your soul sucks things in too. Sometimes, in a bad situation, you may "suck in" an evil spirit. That's not exactly how it happens, but it's a good picture anyway. After you get over being scared, you take a deep breath and blow it out, and that helps you relax. But when it comes to trauma, people often don't deal with it right when it happens. Over the years, the trauma sticks around and grows. Many adults are still dealing with traumatic things that happened when they were your age. That's why I encourage you to deal with any emotional trauma you may have now, instead of letting it hang around twenty years.

How do you deal with emotional trauma? If it was because of someone else, forgive them. Good examples of this are divorce, car wrecks, being left alone, getting locked in somewhere like a car or closet, or almost dying. Moving towns, someone close to you dying, seeing something that scares you, being scared by someone, and hurtful situations can also count as trauma. When you forgive whoever was responsible, don't forget to tell the evil spirit you "sucked in" to leave you. If you don't make it leave, the evil spirit may remind you of the hurt. The enemy may even make you feel the hurt in your body or cause you to dream about it. So get rid of it!

If you did what caused the trauma, apologize to God and repent. Don't forget to forgive yourself. Yep, that's right, forgive yourself. You are Father's child too, and He doesn't like you to mistreat His kids, even if it is you. When you forgive, you also give up the right to punish people for what they've done. You will not even punish yourself. When you punish and want people to hurt or know how badly they hurt you, the healing in your heart isn't finished yet. Remember to let the pain go, and if necessary, let yourself off the hook for it. Jesus does!

Door 4: Inner Vows and Judgments

The fourth door of access for the enemy is the door of Inner Vows and Judgments. The Bible gives us stern warnings about these things.

> *"Judge not, that you be not judged. For with the judgment you pronounce you will be judged, and with the measure you use it will be measured to you."*   Matthew 7:1,2 ESV

> *"Let what you say be simply "Yes" or "No"; anything more than this comes from evil."*   Matthew 5:37 ESV

These verses make it clear that whatever judgments and vows I send out will come back on me. To understand how serious that is, let's see what these words mean.

Inner - means inside of you. It is not something that is visible or specifically to do with other people.

Vow - a promise you make to yourself, someone else, or even God. We usually make vows when we're young, and they can affect us all our lives.

Often times we make vows in reaction to something we don't like. We may say things like, "I'll never drink beer like my dad," or "When I grow up, I'll never miss my child's performance at school." Sentences that begin, "I'll never" or "I'll always" are often good clues that you've made vows. It seems like you're saying a good thing, but what is really happening is you are saying in your heart that you are in control of your whole life. The truth is you don't know what will happen in the future,only Jesus does. Besides, you don't control your life anymore.

Remember, when we give our lives to Jesus, we've been bought, and we are no longer our own. It's not bad to want to do right things, but a vow usually rides alongside with a judgment. What is a judgment you ask?

Judgment - when you decide you know what's in the heart of someone else, usually accompanied with pride or haughtiness in your heart.

Thinking you know what is in the heart of someone else or that you know what they are thinking puts you in the place of God. He is the only one who knows what is truly there. Father can give us words of knowledge about what is going on, but when we base the information on what we think, we're speaking from a human place, not a Godly place. Can you imagine pushing Father off the throne in Heaven and taking over for awhile? Well, in a way, that's what you are doing when you judge.

A judgment raises you up above someone because you think you are better and won't blow it like they have. That sounds like pride to me. It's the same thing Lucifer thought. Yuck! He's not the one you want to agree with. Things didn't work out for him, and if you judge people, they won't work out for you either. You see, Father set things up so that if you judge, you get judged the same way. How can that be? When you step off of the good path Father planned for you, you head out on your own into the unprotected woods.

Imagine judgment as shooting an arrow at someone. In the spirit realm, it is like there is a string tied to the arrow that is attached to you. The enemy gets to work in the place you shot the arrow. That's bad enough, but that same enemy can walk on that string right back to you and work on you too. Curses work this way as well, but we'll get to those later.

Imagine again that judgments are like eye glasses. What if my best friend forgets my birthday? It hurts my feelings, so I make an inner vow and judgment. I may say, "He's so un-thoughtful. He wasn't even thinking of me and only thinks of himself. I will never expect anything from him again so I don't get disappointed." Well, now guess what? Even if he does something wonderful and thoughtful for me, I can't fully receive it or appreciate it because I will see everything he does through the "un-thoughtful" lenses I am wearing. I'll likely decide what was going on in his heart and feel like he could never do enough to repay me for what he'd forgotten before. So he can't make things right with me, and I can't feel better about things. Ugh, we both lose.

But wait, there's more! The Bible says I'll be judged in the same way I judged my friend. Because I've disobeyed Father and stepped off the path of righteousness, the enemy has the right to work me over and make me appear unthoughtful to other people. It may not be exactly like the vow or judgment I made, but it will be similar. For example, I may not be judged for forgetting a birthday, but it will be something in the same neighborhood as that. I might be judged as unthoughtful or mean because I didn't show up for something. I didn't mean to miss it, other things just distracted me. Where do you think the distractions came from? Uhhuh. The enemy set me up! It wasn't in my heart to miss it, I just blew it. But I sure may get judged for it, just like I judged my friend.

On a more serious note, what if child abuse or something ugly like that has led to a judgment? Can Jesus help that too? Of course, nothing is too terrible for Him to forgive or rescue you from. He sees you with love, just like He sees the one doing the sin with love. Nobody wakes up one morning when they are little and decides they want to hurt their children some day. No one ever says, "Gee, when I grow up, I want my kids to be scared of me." It is usually the opposite. People make vows to do something good, and the enemy is empowered through the vows to do something bad.

Never forget that Satan and his demons are evil. Father is good and love and is always working to rescue us. Remember, Jesus gave us the authority to destroy the works of the devil. It is time to quit griping at Father or believing He's bad. It is time for us to live like Jesus paid for us to. It is time to repent, be rescued, be empowered, and go to war for other people.

If you want to stop the pain and ugliness in your life from judgments and vows, pray this or something like this from your heart:

"Father , please forgive me for judging (insert name here, often a parent) _____. Please forgive me for being so prideful and thinking I knew what was in their heart. Only You know that. I forgive them for _____. I renounce the judgment (what you thought and/or said) _____ and destroy the power of those words. Please remove the glasses of judgment from me and show me Your TRUTH. Open my eyes to see them as you see them. Please heal me inside and out. In Jesus' name, any evil spirit that gained access to me through this must leave! Holy Spirit, please fill me up."

Door 5: Curses

Do you believe in blessings? What do you say when someone sneezes? Why is it that people talk all day about blessings and even thank Father for them, but we never hear of curses? I think the enemy has done a good job of making people think that curses are only hocus pocus from the movies. But if we believe blessings are real and for today, why wouldn't curses be the same?

A lot of folks have no idea what a blessing or a curse even is, so let's look at some word meanings here:

Blessing - an empowerment for good, usually spoken. Some blessings have conditions or rules you have to follow to get them. Other blessings you get "just because". Imagine someone painting a target on your back for good things to hit. That's a blessing.

Curse - an empowerment for evil, often spoken. Some curses are allowed to work because of something someone in your family, city, or nation has done. Other curses you bring on yourself. Imagine a target on your back again. This target is for bad things to hit you and your life. That's a curse.

Bowling lanes sometimes have little bumpers that pop out to keep your ball out of the gutter. That's how I think of curses. If my aim is off, my ball bumps alongside them until it gets back on track. I set the ball in motion, and it goes where I caused it to go. The effect is that it bumps back and forth along the sides. It may eventually hit the pins, but it won't knock as many down as it would have if I had rolled the ball straight. The bumpers rob my ball's momentum.

Similarly, many blessings and curses are cause and effect. When you ignore Holy Spirit and go your own way, you are off target and the end result isn't good. You get robbed of some of your power!

As we have discussed, Father, Son, and Holy Spirit created things to work in certain ways. According to God's design, there are basically two worlds, or realms: the seen and the unseen. Each realm has its own set of rules, or ways things work. The realm we see works with things like gravity, time, colors, etc. But the seen realm is really just a kind of copy of the unseen realm.

The unseen world has ways it works too, such as giving, loving, or judging. One of the ways Father lets us know how the unseen realm works is by what He wrote in His Word. When Jesus came, He didn't get rid of how Father made the realms to work. He lived by the rules of both worlds perfectly. We are expected to live by the rules of each realm, too.

> "Do not think I have come to abolish the Law or the Prophets; I have not
> come to abolish them, but to fulfill them. For truly I say to you,
> until heaven and earth pass away, not an iota, not a dot, will
> pass from the Law until all is accomplished." Matthew 5:17-19 ESV

When we blow it and live outside of the ways Father set for us to live, that counts as a cause. The effect is a curse may come into our lives. When a curse is working in our lives, we may feel like that bowling ball, just bouncing back and forth with no real power. But you see, Jesus became cursed for us, so we don't have to suffer the effects of our wrong actions. We can repent and remind the enemy that Jesus already paid the price for the curse we've been living with.

How do you know if you are living under a curse? If these things are happening in your life or your family a lot, there might be a curse:

- Insanity, craziness, depression, confusion
- Diseases or sicknesses passed down through the family
- Trouble having babies or other female problems
- Divorce or division in family relationships
- Can't make or keep money
- Always having accidents
- Suicide
- Unnatural, early, or violent deaths

The good news is the Bible teaches us the reasons why these curses come upon us. Once we know the cause, we can get rid of the effect.

Main Causes of Curses:

1. Disobedience or disrespect for parents

> *"Children, obey your parents in the Lord; for this is right. Honor your father and mother, which is the first commandment with a promise; That it may be well with you, and you may live long on earth."*
>
> Galatians 6:1-3 ESV

Notice, if you obey (there's the cause) you get a good and long life (there's the effect). By using logic, you can know the opposite is true. Disobey or disrespect your parents and your life will not be as long or as good as it was planned to be. You might think that this somehow doesn't apply to you because …blah blah blah. Yep! It surely does apply to you. I know it might be tempting to point out your parents' shortcomings (by the way, this also applies to those acting as parents for you), but here's the deal – Father wrote this knowing that no one would ever have perfect parents. There are no excuses and no exceptions.

By obeying this commandment from Father, you put your trust in Him. You are having faith in Father God rather than your parents. He is the one who made the promise of blessing, so He's really who you are dealing with here. The issue is not whether your parents are correct or if they deserve to be obeyed. The issue is whether or not you will obey God! Now, don't get me wrong – if your parents are instructing you to break the law or harm yourself or someone else, Father God knows what's going on, and He will lead you in what to do. Other than that, we are instructed to honor God by obeying our parents. By the way, "harm" doesn't include grounding you, spanking you appropriately, etc.

Many, many demons I've had to cast out of people came in through this specific door. No lie. So, many times I deal with adults who suffer from all of the curses I mentioned before because they didn't understand that their disobedience was to Father God, not their parents. C'mon, people! If you are going to reach a generation and change the world, you must respect the first authorities God puts in your life. If you can't learn to obey and honor the people He used to create you, how will you honor and obey a Father you can't always see or feel?

If you have blown it here, repent. Ask Holy Spirit to deliver you and destroy the curse over your life. Obey Holy Spirit as He teaches you what honor and respect look like.

Another way the unseen realm works is what's called sowing and reaping. That means what you plant is what grows and comes back to you. If you sow/plant respect and honor, soon you receive respect and honor. God doesn't lie, and He promises this works. Put your faith in Him and give it a shot for a while.

For those places your parents are falling short, forgive them. You may even need to repent to them and bring this stuff up to the light. God gives us our parents from His perfect heart as a blessing and to show us a little bit of what He's like. But just like the rest of God's beautiful plan, the enemy tries to slime it. If the enemy can mess up your picture of an earthly father, you will have a messed up view of our perfect heavenly Father. If the enemy can mess up your relationship with your mom, you may have a hard time understanding the tender, nurturing side of God. Remember God isn't a man, or a woman. He's neither and both. He created both in His image, so there's both the mom side and the dad side to Him.

Forgive your parents; close the doors we've talked about in the spirit. Let Father heal you and change how you think and how you experience Him.

2. Paying too much attention to or worshipping other gods

One reason God made us is to worship Him. If we worship other false gods, we're setting ourselves up for trouble. Enough said.

3. Involvement with the occult or witchcraft

Yep, this is the part where I talk about Harry Potter. You are reading this manual and waking up to the things of the spirit at a time on this planet when God is revealing more of Himself than ever before. People who don't even have a clue about God as their Father are picking up on the increase in the focus on supernatural things. Haven't you noticed how many wizards, vampires, witches and weirdos are in movies and on TV? It is all about the source. Let me say it again, it is all about the source.

There are only two sources of power in our lives. Good comes from Father and evil comes from Satan. Pretty simple. So, if you can't figure out where the power comes from, stay away from it. If you aren't sure, ask Holy Spirit or someone who knows Holy Spirit really well.

In the coming days, "powers" and supernatural things will increase. You can become slaves of the losers with evil power or well equipped warriors for the King of all kings. Do not mess around with anything that even gives you a yucky feeling in your gut. That's Holy Spirit warning you. Listen. Just checking witchcraft out or watching it opens a door. If you've been involved in witchcraft or any power that's not from Father, repent, get delivered, and let Jesus heal you. By the way, there are NO good wizards, witches, etc. It is all about source.

4. Taking advantage of or hurting those weaker than you

5. All sexual relationships that are out of line with what Father says

6. Dishonoring God's chosen people

This involves Israelites who were born Jewish. God loves those folks and you should too. Don't even joke or laugh at jokes about Jewish people. Just so you know, Jesus was Jewish. Your spiritual roots are Jewish. The church didn't replace Israel, and if you bless Israel, you get blessed. Duh. Pray for Jewish people to recognize that Jesus is the Messiah for whom they are waiting. Pray for Israel to be protected and in peace.

7. Depending on human strength instead of God

8. Stealing and lying

9. Not tithing or giving

Tithing - giving 10% or more of your money to whoever teaches/feeds you spiritually

Basically, God gives you every good thing you have. He wants to give you a chance to show Him how thankful you are by giving money. The love of money is the root of all kinds of bad stuff. If you will give it back to God and remember that it is Him who supplies what you need, money loses its power over you. So, you can have 90% of your money and have it all blessed or have 100% of it and have all of it cursed.

10. Words spoken over you by people in authority

This includes words spoken by grandparents, parents, teachers, pastors, older siblings, and people like that. We are created in God's image and given great power and responsibility. Father used words to create everything on the planet. That means our words have power, too. What do you use words to create-targets for good or for evil? If you've been cursed or targeted by someone in authority over your life, guess what? Jesus' authority is higher than theirs, and what He says about you is what is real and true. Forgive those who curse you and renounce any partnership you have had in making the curse come true. In Jesus' name, destroy the power of those words over you and destroy the assignments/arrows of evil over your life. Now, bless those who curse you and see amazing things happen!

11. Negative, empty words you've spoken against yourself

Oftentimes, people say things about themselves when they're hurt, discouraged, or angry. When you do that, you are cursing yourself. Guess what? Even those words with which you curse yourself while you are mumbling under your breathe count. Examples of this are "I'm so stupid," "I'm never going to make it," "I'll always be this way," "I get a cold every January," etc.

The Bible says every word you speak begins in your heart-every single word. So, even if think you are joking around and you "don't really mean it," the truth is that deep down you actually do mean it. Repent for cursing yourself and agreeing with the enemy. Ask Holy Spirit why it is in your heart and what you need to do to get it out.

12. Promises or agreements taken to join ungodly secret societies

The fact that a club or organization has to be kept secret is a big hint that its source is wrong! Hello! If it was good, why would they want it kept secret? One very well known "secret society" is the Freemasons. Shriners are another. Most of the men who join this organization don't realize what they are getting into. They are often Godly men who just don't have all of the information because most of it is kept secret! If you know of this in your family line, forgive your forefathers and repent for it being in your family. Demand every spirit be kicked out and leave you, in Jesus' name. Do not join up if you are ever asked.

13. Curses pronounced on you by those in the occult or witchcraft

Finally the one everyone knows about – or do you? This can include cultural things. Hispanic people go to "healers" or curanderos. African and Indian people go to witch doctors or traditional doctors. Some people go to raiki or natural energy healers. Gee, what's the source? The earth was created by God and not Mother Nature or Father Time! If God used a plant to make healing chemicals, would you worship the plant or the creator of the plant? The Bible says some people worship created things and not the creator. Yup, that's what a lot of that is. Crystals don't heal you and magnets don't love you. Don't be a chump! Worship the Master and Creator of all things. Why bother with lesser things?

14 .Cheap talk about others while pretending to be lead by the Holy Spirit

This happens when we gossip about others, but pretend it is for their good. It can also happen when you pretend you are just getting the facts straight and you seek out more information. This can happen anywhere – the lunchroom, locker room, before school, and even at church.

15. Witchcraft Prayers

Witchcraft is a pretty bad word to combine with prayers. That's what it is when you seek to control another person or situation while praying apart from Holy Spirit. While you pray, let your heart be tender to how the Holy Spirit wants to guide you to pray. Don't try to manipulate or get you own way by slapping the cover of prayer on what you're saying. Blaming other people and accusations fall under this category, too. When you pray, remember that you are talking to a Holy God, and that His will is what is important.

So there you have it: a list of many of the main reasons curses come into our lives. The good news is that Jesus stepped in and took the curses upon Himself so we didn't have to. Read Isaiah 53 and Galatians 6. He took them all, so there's no reason to keep letting them work!

If you ask, Holy Spirit will show you where curses are working in your life. After He shows you, repent, forgive, and pray something like this:

"Father in Jesus' Name, I destroy the curses over my life. I see where the enemy has stolen from me and I ask you to send the angels to get it all back for me. Every spirit that has worked in, on, or through my life must leave now. Holy Spirit, angels, rescue me. Fill me up and minister to me please."

Questions for Chapter Four

1. "Are they not all ministering spirits, _____
   _____." Hebrews 1:14

2. Rescue from evil or Deliverance is part of Sozo Salvation. T/F

3. The two major doors by which demons enter are: 1) Intrusion
   2)_____.

4. The five doors of legal ground are: 1) _____
   2) Unforgiveness 3) Emotional _____ 4) Inner _____
   and Judgments 5) _____.

5. Jesus came to get rid of the Old Testament. T/F

Chapter Five:
Know Your Enemy -
Root Spirits

Have you ever tried to quit doing something you knew was wrong? Sometimes you can, and other times you can't. You think you've got the fight won and next thing you know, boom! You fall and do it again.

Trust me; I've done that, too. When I lost those battles, I would get really down on myself. I blamed my own weaknesses for the fall. However, I eventually found out it wasn't always my fault that I failed. There was something pushing me toward that thing I knew I shouldn't do. What a huge relief to discover it wasn't all me! So, who was helping me fail and who was I really fighting?

Ephesians 4:25 says, "Be angry and do not sin; do not let the sun go down on your anger, and give no opportunity to the devil." In this verse, "opportunity" is also translated "place." That means that a devil, or evil spirit, can have a place to work in me if I let it. Does that help you see what is happening sometimes when you sin?

As we think about what happens, let's remember there's more to this world than we can see with our eyes. If the future of your life were visible, it might look like a road map. At this moment it would read, "You are here." You are not near the end of the trip, but you aren't at the very beginning either. It is your mission to travel across the territory, keep the lands you pass through safe, and take over new lands. There is a lot of territory for you to cover before you finish, and there are places and things out there that don't want you to finish your mission well.

The enemy has been given control of a lot of the territories through the five doors we talked about earlier. Not only do the enemy troops move in, but they also build forts. If they have a fort to keep them safe, it is harder for you to defeat them. Fortunately for you, we've been given supernatural weapons for pulling down the forts and kicking the enemy out of our turf.

We'll get to the enemy troops later, but first let's look at their forts. What are the forts made of? Feelings, thoughts, and patterns of behavior are like the bricks and mortar that hold the fort together. Imagine you see something sexy and it creates a feeling. Experiencing the feeling again will draw you to it. You can literally feel yourself being pulled. Those feelings are like the mortar or glue. Doing something active to get more of that feeling is like a brick. Put enough bricks together with enough mortar and it forms a place for the enemy to live and work.

For example, you've accidentally seen the sexy thing once. Now, suppose you choose to go back to where you saw it so you can get that feeling again. You may begin to believe it isn't that bad to look at that thing you saw. If someone asks you about it, you may lie. Well, guess what, friend? If these things are happening, you have a fort, or stronghold of the enemy, in your territory.

You may have been influenced by the feelings and lies of something other than yourself, but you agreed with it. It takes the power of God and His truth to destroy the forts the enemy builds. When you hear, see, or receive revelation of truth, it will smash the bricks of the enemy to powder. Once you know the truth, it will make you free.

So, by what were you influenced when you helped build the stronghold? Fallen angels, demon spirits, unclean spirits, and other ugly dudes are the guilty parties. I won't go into details about the differences between these things, but whatever you call them, they are real. I'll just call them all spirits from now on.

The Bible discusses spirits from the beginning to the end. They're mentioned everywhere you look. And just like the truths of the Bible don't change, the main characters don't either.

A lot of people have believed several ideas about spirits that are simply not true. One idea suggests spirits are just thought patterns in your head. Another idea claims that spirits are always invisible, and you will never feel or see them. Some people say if you just ignore a spirit long enough, it will leave. Many people believe these kinds of things and more about spirits, but the Bible teaches otherwise.

According to the Bible, our ultimate source of truth, a spirit is not the same as a way of thinking, and spirits are not "just in your mind." You may not always see spirits or feel them, but sometimes you will. A spirit will not leave you alone just because you ignore it. To deal with evil spirits, you must take the authority Jesus died to give you, close the open doors that let them in, and tell them to leave in Jesus' mighty name!

Why learn all this about spirits? The Bible tells us not to be ignorant of how the enemy works so we can defeat him. For too long, Christians have been too fearful to catch on to what the devil does. He lies to you, devises evil plans, and makes things seem bigger than they really are. That's because he's scared of you and he's trying to take you out! So just like doctors study diseases to figure out how they work, we look at the enemy and figure out ways to beat him.

Remember, Jesus defeated Satan and took away the power of the enemy over you. Holy Spirit brings us truth, shows us God's plan, and reveals the true size of things. God is big; Satan is not. It's all about our focus. We don't ignore the dark side, but our focus stays on God.

Think of the government workers who are in charge of making sure fake money isn't going around. They don't focus on all of the possible fake dollars out there. They just know the real dollar so well they can tell if something isn't right.

That's how we are supposed to be. We should know Holy Spirit so well that anything not like Him is obvious to us. At the same time, focusing on the real dollar doesn't make all the fake ones go away. When we come across a spirit that isn't Holy Spirit, we take it to the trash just like the government officials do with fake money.

> *"Every tree that does not bear good fruit is cut down and thrown into the fire. Thus you will know them by their fruits."*   Matthew 7:19-20 ESV

I want you to be equipped to recognize the fruit or evidence of the enemy at work. If you know these spirits well, you will know what's going on in the spiritual realm by little hints they accidentally give away through actions, physical expressions, words, or just a knowing in your gut. When you see the evidence that they are at work, you can kick them out of your life and territory.

Soon, you'll get good at kicking bad spirits out of your life, and you can help other people kick them out. When you help one person, you can help many. How about a whole family getting cleaned out of evil spirits and filled up with Holy Spirit? When you rescue many from evil, you can change a city, a state, a nation – even the whole world!

That's what this is all about. First, you recognize the enemy's strongholds in your territory. Then you use truth and repentance to tear down the forts, those sinful patterns of thinking, feeling, and acting. Once you tear down his house, you kick the enemy out of your territory. Finally, you start helping other people get free like you are.

Let's take a look at the bad guys living in those places and the fruit they produce. To help believers recognize them, a man named Dr. Henry Malone, who is really great at kicking spirits out of people's lives, came up with a list of basic kinds of spirits. These are not all the spirits, but these are some of the main ones. They're called root spirits because lots of common fruits can be traced back to them. It's kind of like a tree. It may have lots of branches, with tons of different fruit, but all the branches grow from the roots. If you cut the roots, all the branches die. Similarly, if we cut the spiritual roots by the power of Holy Spirit, the bad fruit dies. Remember we learn about spirits, but we focus on Holy Spirit.

Additionally, a friend of mine drew pictures of what these spirits may look like to help you remember what and whom you are fighting. For all I know, he was really seeing these things and just thought he was imagining what they looked like. Anyway, don't get carried away with what these wimps look like, but do get familiar with their fruits.

A word of warning here: Some guys in the Bible heard about rescuing people from evil spirits and decided to try it. They were actually very well educated in the Bible of that time, but they didn't know Jesus or have Holy Spirit inside to empower them. When they tried to cast a spirit out of a guy, all of them got beaten up and kicked out of the house naked! Check out Acts 19 for the official version.

If you know of any open doors in your life or are choosing to sin, do not try to kick anything out of anyone else's life.   You must be in a very close, loving friendship with Father, Jesus, and Holy Spirit to do these things. The enemy is a defeated wimp, but he is still evil, and he would love to destroy your life if you give him any chance.

NOTE: Each spirit's name is underlined, followed by Scripture references to show where that spirit is found in the Bible. The fruits they produce are listed after each Scripture.

<u>Infirmity</u>

> *"And behold, there was a woman who had a spirit of infirmity eighteen years, and was bowed together and could in no wise lift herself."*
>
> Luke 13:11 KJV

Allergies
Arthritis
Asthma
Attacks on womanhood/manhood: "You are gay," "You'll never be a real man/woman," etc.
Cancer
Diabetes
Female problems
Fevers
Fungus
Heart disease
High blood pressure
Always sick
Sinus
Stroke
Viruses
Weakness/feebleness

INFIRMITY

DIVINATION

Divination

"And it came to pass, as we went to prayer, a certain damsel possessed with a spirit of divination met us, which brought her masters much gain by soothsaying." Acts 16:16 KJV

Astrology - interpreting the stars (not astronomy - study of the stars)
Channeling-letting a spirit use your body
Crystal balls/8 balls   Fortune tellers
Mediums - letting a dead person's spirit speak through you
Demonic games (Dungeons &Dragons, Pokémon)
Horoscopes   Rebellion   Stubbornness
Independence - "I don't need anyone else. I'll do it myself."
Hypnosis   Ouija boards   Palm readers   Satanism, Wicca
Mutterer   Séances   Mysticism
Tarot cards, Goddess cards   Witchcraft   Drugs
Transcendental meditation - Hindu meditation
Manipulation - getting your way by lying, silence, crying, anger etc.
Freemasonry- a secret club that looks like it does good, but is evil at higher levels.   All Freemasonry is bad.
Trying to do deliverance that isn't Biblical
Migraine Headaches-terrible headaches where light hurts your eyes and you get sick

Ahab

"And Ahab the son of Omri did evil in the sight of the LORD, more than all who were before him."   **1 Kings 16:30 KJV**
Wimpy   Pouter   Gets what it wants by using power of other people
Where there is an Ahab, there is a Jezebel. Ahab acts like child, Jezebel acts like parent.

Jezebel

"Then Jezebel sent a messenger to Elijah, saying, "So may the gods do to me and more also, if I do not make your life as the life of one of them by this time tomorrow."   **1 Kings 19:2 KJV**
Controlling   Prideful   Religious   Threatening with words,
looks, actions   Uses people to get what it wants   Manipulative - "works it" to
get what it wants

Python

"As we were going to the place of prayer, we were met by a slave girl who had a spirit of divination and brought her owners much gain by fortune-telling."

Acts 16:16 KJV

Deut. 18:10-12   Numbers 22:7 Divination   Witchcraft
Addictions   Drugs   Over the counter drugs
Apathy - you just don't care anymore Prov. 29:18   Infirmity/death
Control   Heaviness   Depression
Suicide - killing yourself or trying to kill yourself
Attempts to 'squeeze' the life out of individual
Destroys excitement about your mission in life

Whoredom

"They will not frame their doings to turn to their God; for the spirit of whoredoms is in the midst of them, and they have not known the LORD."

Hosea 5:4 KJV

Sex with someone you are not married to
Showing off your body
Illegitimacy - born to parents who aren't married. This is also a curse
Sexual relationships within a family
Lust   Masturbation - sex by yourself, touching yourself sexually
Molestation - wrong touching or sex with a child
Molested as a child   Secretly watching other people
Pornography - watching or reading about sex in an ungodly way
Sex-texting   Rape Seduction - tempting or attraction to you in a wrong way. Flirting can eventually go here.
Harlotry - paying or trading for sex, prostitute, chasing after other lovers
All sexual sins   Idolatry - love of money, possessions, position, popularity, power, etc. Or worship of anything other than God

Fear

"For God hath not given us the spirit of fear; but of power, and of love and of a sound mind."
2 Timothy1:7 KJV

Abandonment - being left alone
Anxiety
Worry
Critical spirit - criticize everything, negative
Faithlessness
Fright
Inadequacy - "I can't do it"
Inferiority - not good enough, smart enough, good looking, etc.
Insanity - crazy
Migraines
Nightmares
Performance/Perfectionism -"I have to do it well to be loved or accepted"
Phobias- really strong fear that is out of balance with reality, for example: fear of heights
Rejection/fear of rejection
Self-rejection/Self Hate
Shyness
Muscle tightness always
Stress (heart attack)
Timidity
Torment
Schizophrenia - diagnosed as a disease where you often hear voices
Paranoia - thinking everyone is looking at you, talking about you, after you
Idleness - scared to do anything
Lack of trust
Fear of death, pain, failure, poverty, men/women, others' opinions, success, authority, etc.

Anti-Christ (against the anointing)

"And every spirit that confesseth not that Jesus Christ is come in the flesh is not from God: and this is that spirit of antichrist, whereof ye have heard that it should come; and even now already is in the world."

1 John 4:3 KJV

Denies the Holy Spirit & gifts
Against the Bible
Explains away the power of God-no more miracles
Opposes Christ as God, His Victory over Satan & that He was human too
Attempts to take the place of Christ
Bullies the saints
Kills the saints for what they believe
Causes church splits
Gives up on Christianity
Judaism - Jewish people who don't believe Jesus is the Messiah

JEALOUSY

Jealousy

*"**And the spirit of jealousy come upon him, and he be jealous of his wife, and she be defiled; or the spirit of jealousy come upon him and she be not defiled:**"*

Numbers 5:14 KJV

Anger, wrath, rage, murder
Unnatural competition
Covetousness - want what other people have
Cruelty
Distrustful
Divorce/division
Feels God loves others more than themselves
Hatred
Jealousy
Insecurity
Revenge
Self-centeredness
Suspicion
Hard-heartedness
Builds walls in person's life - won't let people close to their heart
Abortion - cares more about themselves than the baby

Bondage

"Ye have not received the spirit of bondage again to fear; but ye have received the Spirit of adoption, whereby we cry, Abba, Father." Romans 8:15 KJV

Addicted to possessions
Alcohol
Anorexia/bulimia - not eating to be skinny/ eating and then throwing up
Cigarettes
Co-dependency - overboard friendships when it is out of balance and one controls the other
Work
Computers
Internet
Pornography
Drugs
Food
TV
Video games
Sex
Soul ties
Superiority - addicted to self
Wishing you had what someone else has so you could keep it all to yourself

PRIDE

Haughtiness

"Pride goeth before destruction, and an haughty spirit before a fall. Better it is to be of an humble spirit with the lowly, than to divide the spoil with the proud."

Proverbs 16:18-19 KJV

Arrogance
Boastful - bragging
Contentious - always in an argument
Controlling
Critical
Extremely bossy
Proud - it's all about me
Gossip - talking about other people even if it is true
Judgmental -"I'm better than them. I would never do that"
Prejudice - thinking one culture, race or male or female is better
Mockery
Rudeness
Self-righteousness - "I behave well and don't have anything wrong with me"
Superiority - better than everyone else
Vanity - overly concerned with appearance or things that don't really matter
Indifference -"I don't care about your feelings or stuff"
Overbearing - always wants things their way
Scorn - thinking badly of people
Lofty looks - looking down on people
Stubbornness

Error

"We are of God; he that knoweth God heareth us; he that is not of God heareth not us. Hereby know we the spirit of truth and the spirit of error."   1 John 4:6 KJV

Anorexia , bulimia - not eating to be skinny or eating and then throwing up

Compromise - never taking a stand, always playing the middle man, agreeing even when you don't

Confusion

Continuously make wrong decisions

Cults/false doctrine

False teachers/ prophets/preachers

False tongues

Doubt/unbelief

Deception

Immaturity

Irresponsibility

Inappropriate thinking/ behavior

Anti-Semitism - against Jewish people

Intellectualism - have to understand to believe

HEAVINESS

Heaviness

"To appoint unto them to console all who mourn in Zion, to give unto them beauty for ashes, the oil of joy for mourning, the garment of praise for the spirit of heaviness; that they might called trees of righteousness, the planting of the Lord, that he might be glorified." Isaiah 61:3 KJV

Abnormal grieving - can't get over a loss, (example: Grandma died and you cry for months)
Defilement - feel dirty
Depression
Discouragement
Hopelessness
Loneliness
Continual sadness
Self-pity
Shame
Unjustified guilt
Wounded spirit
Continual sorrow
Rejection
Humiliation
Whining
Broken heartedness
Gloominess
Often dress in Goth and have hair covering their face
Shame - people often hide their face until the spirit leaves
Think of Eeyore from Winnie the Pooh books

Lying

"Now therefore, behold, the Lord has put a lying spirit in the mouth of thy prophets, and the Lord hath spoken evil against thee." *2 Chronicles 18:22 KJV*

Condemnation - always feeling guilty
Deception
Exaggeration
Flattery - fake compliments
Excessive talking
Hypocrisy - say one thing and do another
Lies
Emotionalism - using emotions to get your way
Profanity - cursing, using bad language, never treating anything with honor or as special
Vain imaginations - imagining a whole situation before you get there or say something
Religious spirit
Lies about God
Performance/Perfectionism - I have to do it well to be loved or accepted
Financial problems (if one is tithing and still has them)
Poor self image: "You're ugly", "stupid", "worthless", "never marry", "no one wants you", "you'll never change", "fat", "whore", "liar", etc

Deaf and Dumb

"When Jesus saw that the people came running together, he rebuked the foul spirit, saying unto him, "Though dumb and deaf spirit, I charge thee, come out of him, and enter no more into him. And the spirit cried, and rent him sore, and came out of him: And he was as one dead' insomuch that many said, He is dead. But Jesus took him by the hand, and lifted him up: and he arose."   Mark 9:25-27 KJV

Accidents with drowning/fire
Convulsions
Diseases of eyes/ears
Epilepsy
Grinding teeth
Insanity
Seizure
Stupor - to act like your brain is numb or you can't feel anything
Suicidal thoughts and attempts
Schizophrenia
Inappropriate and excessive crying
Deafness

Perverseness/Twisted

"The Lord hath mingled a perverse spirit in the midst thereof; and they have caused Egypt to err in every work thereof, as a drunk man staggereth in his vomit."

Isaiah 19:14 KJV

False teachers/doctrine
Homosexuality/Gay
Twisted thinking
Polygamy - married to more than one person
Liking to hurt or be hurt
Sexual deviations
Error (especially in religious areas)
Unreasonableness
Abnormal crankiness
Self lovers
Stubbornness
Twists Bible verses to get what you want or hurt people

PERVERSITY

Sleep/Stupor

"According as it is written, God hath given them the spirit of stupor ; eyes that they should not see, and ears that they should not hear; unto this very day."

Romans 11:8 KJV

Constant fatigue - always tired
Draws back from life
Human spirit is asleep
Wish you have never been born
Passivity/Wimp
"Wallflower"
Self-pity
Procrastination - waiting until the last minute
Success blocked

Death

Death isn't called a spirit in the Bible, but it can act like one, and it certainly is a curse.

> *"Forasmuch then as the children are partakers of flesh and blood, he also himself took part of the same; that through death he might destroy him that had the power of death, that is, the devil; and deliver them who through fear of death were all their lifetime subject to bondage."*
> Hebrews 2:14-15 KJV

Near death accidents
Near-drowning
Death curses, especially by parents
Abortion
Suicide attempts
Freemasonry
(Not necessarily a root spirit, but works closely with them.)

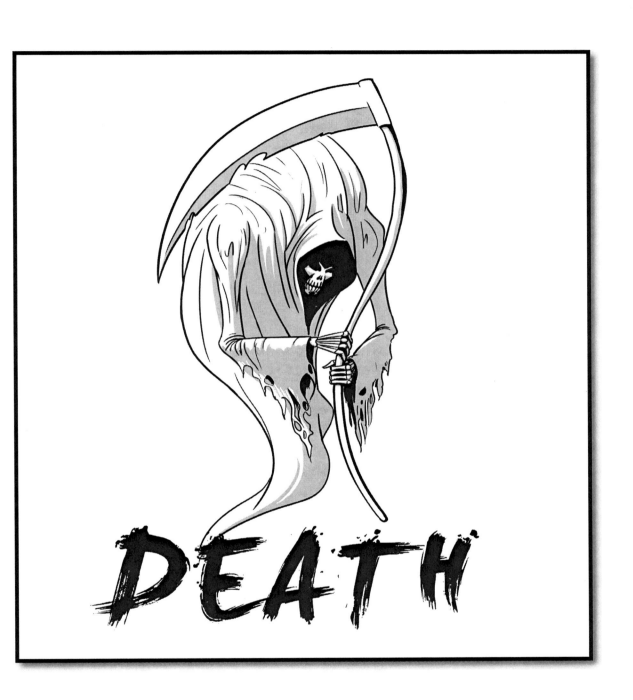

Now that you are familiar with these slime balls, let's get rid of them. The power to throw them out isn't from you or even someone you are with. It is Jesus' empowerment that destroys the hold of the enemy. One touch from God can change everything.

Deliverance cannot be something you just do or say and don't mean from your heart. I recommend getting with a mature saint with spiritual authority who knows about deliverance ministry. Spirits often show up in different ways, and you want to be with someone who knows what to do! Some people feel dizzy, sick to their stomachs, nervous, or they begin coughing, choking, crying, or yawning. Some people don't feel anything, and others just sigh a lot. Remember, it isn't about what you do or don't feel or see. However, there will be a sense of release or peace. When something leaves, remember to ask Holy Spirit to fill you up there. You don't want your soul to be full of holes like Swiss cheese.

When you find someone you trust, follow Holy Spirit, and He will likely take you through something like this:

1.   **Are you a Christian? If you aren't, you won't stay free because you don't have the authority or power to stay free. You will end up worse than before. Matt. 12:43**
2.   **Give God all control over you and depend on Him to free you.**
3.   **Take away all legal ground for the enemy to stay by closing all open doors in the spirit. This is like the repenting we did earlier in the manual. If you need to forgive someone, do it. If you need to repent on behalf of those in your family before you, do that. Go through each root spirit and one-by-one renounce any forts or strongholds they live in, repent for participating with that spirit, and renounce all of the fruits listed. Holy Spirit will add more detail if you need it.**
4.   **Command each spirit you renounced to leave you, one-by-one or in groups, as Holy Spirit leads you. Don't worry about every name of everything unless Holy Spirits says you need to. If you aren't sure what spirit or group it fits in, just call it by what it makes you feel. For example, if it makes you feel ugly, just tell the "spirit of ugly" to leave you. The release of peace will be there when it goes.**
5.   **Thank God and praise Him for freeing you! The next chapter on Intimacy with Christ will rock this!**

Questions for Chapter Five

Fill in the blanks.

1.   Enemy forts are made of _____ and thoughts.

2.   Demon spirits are really just ways of thinking. T/F

3.   You can sometimes identify Root Spirits by their _____.

4.   The Root Spirits listed in this chapter are all there are. T/F

5.   List the Root Spirits and at least one fruit of its presence:
        1._____: fruit- Cancer
        2. Divination a) python b) Jezebel c) Ahab _____
        3.Whoredom: _____
        4. _____: nightmares
        5. Anti-_____ : denies Holy Spirit and gifts
        6. Jealousy: _____
        7. Bondage :_____
        8._____ : pride
        9. Error: _____
        10. Heaviness :_____
        11. _____:"you're ugly."
        12. _____ and Dumb: accidents
        13.Perversity: _____
        14. Sleep/Stupor: _____

Chapter Six:
Intimacy with Christ

You probably know someone who has a crush on someone else. They follow that person around acting cool, trying to say funny things, and probably looking a little silly along the way. They try really hard to get that person's attention, and when they finally do get that person to look their way, they feel like they're on top of the world!

You may want to sit down before I tell you this. Are you ready? Here goes. The Creator of the Universe has a crush on you! That's right. God is in love with you. When you give Him your full attention, you have an incredible effect on Father's feelings.

Throughout the Bible, Father reveals HIS passion for HIS people. He called Moses his friend. Enoch pleased God so much, He just took the guy straight home to Heaven. Jesus laughed, cried, rejoiced, and was even betrayed by a friend. And He hasn't changed. If you believe Jesus was raised from the dead, then it only makes sense that He is still alive. If that's true, then He still behaves the same way, right? He is the living God. He remains the same yesterday, today, and forever, and He deeply desires for us to know Him.

Jesus prayed in John 17 that we would know Him and that we would be with Him where He is. Jesus wanted us to know we are as loved by Him as He is by Father. Now you may think, "Of course He loves me, He's God. He has to love me." But did you know Jesus likes you? My dear friend, He enjoys you and wants to be with you.

Jesus sent His Spirit because He wanted to restore the closeness our family lost in the Garden of Eden. The relationship Adam and Eve had with Father has now been given to us. Holy Spirit tells us things from Jesus, and we communicate with Him on a first name basis. We get to spend our lives as Christians knowing God more and more.

The process of growing closer with Father is called intimacy. Intimacy is a word that describes the kind of relationship a husband has with a wife. It can also mean deep, deep friendship. Imagine your best friend. You share your closest secrets, your wildest dreams, and your most intense feelings. In a nutshell, intimacy is a special kind of relationship that involves knowing each other extremely well.

For a long time, I thought knowing about Jesus was the same as knowing Him intimately. I read the Bible to know how to behave better and what to do in certain situations. While those things are useful, they weren't really enough to keep me radically committed to my Savior like I am now. Heck, even the guys who killed Jesus had most of the Bible at that time memorized! They knew how to behave well, but they sure didn't recognize the Lord. Jesus taught again and again that knowing Him and being with Him were the most important things. He even said that knowing God was eternal life! Written as a math equation, it would look like this: Knowing God = Eternal Life. Chew on that one for a while.

Every time I encounter or personally experience Father, Jesus, or Holy Spirit, I am changed. It isn't always something I can put into words, but my actions and heart show the difference. Real intimacy with God will always produce fruit.

So how can we grow our intimacy with Father, Jesus, and Holy Spirit? Of course the answer is pray and read your Bible. You knew that. But there is more. Remember, Jesus prayed that you could be with Him. He has connections, and His prayers are always answered. Jesus wants you to experience Him, so He made it possible for you to be with Him every moment of every day.

Here are some ways we can experience Jesus:

What if you just sat still and thought about Him? What if you just imagined yourself in a Bible story, sitting with Him in your room, or imagined what Heaven is like? What you are doing is meditating on Him, and that is one of the ways we get to know Him better. Weird gurus aren't the only ones who meditate. To meditate simply means to concentrate on something. Concentrating on Jesus helps us understand more of who He is.

There have been times when I wondered what it would be like to wash Jesus' feet or help Him do laundry when He was on earth. When I thought about Him these ways, I would really feel Him in the room with me. Jesus said He wanted to show Himself to those who obey Him. He's not a liar, so I am eagerly waiting for the day I actually see Him. It doesn't have to be when I die. I know a girl who saw Jesus sitting on her bed in her room and talked with Him before she even believed in Him as her Savior! It's exciting to think, "That could be me!" But whether you physically see Jesus or not, He comes near us when our thoughts are focused on Him.

It is important to know the Bible so you have something accurate to think about. It won't do any good to think about Jesus in ways that are not true or that do not honor Him. You also need to be able to compare anything that happens to you with what happened in the Bible. Satan loves to act like God, and he may send spirits to confuse you and fake you out. If you know the Bible, you will recognize whether or not what you experience lines up with what Father has done before or if it is the type thing He would do or say.

You can also test to see if what you are encountering is from Holy Spirit. Say something like the following: "To the spirit who just told me that, do you worship and obey Jesus Christ as your Lord and Savior and worship Him and Him alone? Tell me now, in Jesus' name." If you hear a definite "yes," it is from Holy Spirit. Or you may hear nothing definite but feel a sense of peace. That is most likely Holy Spirit, too. Other times, when you ask the question you might get something freaky or an instant bad feeling. That should tell you where it's coming from. Using this question will usually help you figure out whether what you experience is from Jesus or the other side. However, it is still a good idea to share what's going on with someone in spiritual authority over you, such as a youth leader or someone who is teaching and discipling you.

Another way I often encounter Jesus is during times of worship. Whether it's just me and my iPod on the roads of the ranch, or if I'm in a building full of people, worship is a special time. Worship is like building a place for God to sit down and rest among us. Don't limit it to just singing songs. Worship can be the typical singing situation, but it can also take place through art, dance, writing, movement, or whatever else Holy Spirit prompts you to do to honor God. Just make a big deal of Father. See if you can make Him blush because you are making such a big deal about Him.

When I worship, I focus my mind on Jesus, and He often takes me into visions or imaginations with Him. I love it when I find out something I was just thinking about is real or in the Bible and I didn't know it. One time I "imagined" myself in a temple in a city with a lot of people. There were a lot of details to it. A little while later I heard someone read a verse from the Bible that described exactly what I'd imagined! Whoa! It was like I was in the verse. You can bet I don't have to try hard to remember that verse.

If you don't know how to get close to Father, look around for someone who does. Ask them questions. Do what they do until you figure out what you like to do. It's not wrong to copy the way others get close to God while you're learning how to do it yourself. If you just start pursuing intimacy with Father, you will grow your own special things with Him. It doesn't have to take hours and hours poring over a Bible, unless that's what you like. It can be as simple as a moment of sitting still and imagining blowing Him a kiss, giving Him a loving punch in the arm, or winking at Him across the room.

A story in the Bible compares intimacy to oil in lamps. They used lamps at the time to light things up. If you want to light things up in your life or others' lives, you need oil. Oil is often symbolic of Holy Spirit. Spend time with Him, worship Him, and learn from Him. Your time and depth of connecting with Him will represent the oil in your lamp. The amount of oil you have determines how bright your lamp shines. Make sure when Jesus comes back, He doesn't have to search for you in the dark. May He find you in blazing light with many others around you.

Questions for Chapter Six

1. In what chapter of the book of John does Jesus pray that we would know Him, be with Him, and know we are as loved by the Father as He is?_____--

2. _____ is another word for concentrating on something.

3. Name two ways you can know Jesus better. _____ _____

4. It is good to copy others to learn at first. T/F

5. _____ is symbolic of Holy Spirit.

Chapter Seven:
Seven Spirits of God

I love this chapter of the manual because it is somewhat new to me, and it is flat-out awesome! This is another one of those things I never knew about. Todd Bentley and Keith Miller are two men of God from whom I have learned a lot of this. You may also want to learn from what they teach. As I've learned about the Seven Spirits of God, it has transformed my walk with Jesus, and it will transform yours as well.

You see, God reveals different things about Himself to every generation. It is called progressive revelation. He doesn't change; He just lets us see more of Him. As we get closer to the end of the age, He continues to give us what we need to accomplish His plans for our time.

One revelation God has given His people is the understanding of the Seven Spirits of God. Chapters four and five of the book of Revelation and Isaiah 11:2 all speak of the Seven Spirits of God. They aren't really seven different Spirits, but different functions or activities of the Holy Spirit (kind of like the three-in-one thing with Father, Jesus, and Holy Spirit). In other words, these are seven ways Holy Spirit demonstrates the power and character of God Almighty.

The Bible refers to the Seven Spirits as the Spirit Upon, Spirit of Wisdom, Spirit of Revelation, Spirit of Counsel, Spirit of Might, and Spirit of Knowledge and the Fear of the Lord. Jesus walked with Holy Spirit in the fullness of all of these characteristics 24/7. You and I want that to be the case, but most of the time we concentrate on one or two at a time. That's okay because every expression of Holy Spirit empowers us to walk closer and more powerfully with God. Here's a brief description of what it is like to walk under the empowerment or anointing of each one.

Spirit of the Lord Upon -

This reminds me of Luke 4 where Jesus explains what He was doing on earth. The Spirit of the Lord came upon Jesus to enable Him to preach the gospel and bring Heaven to earth. The same Spirit empowers us to do those things too. Luke 4:18.

The Spirit of Wisdom -

This is not only having the information you need, but knowing what to do with the information. It is like hearing from Holy Spirit something special about someone and then using what you know to really bless them. The Spirit of Wisdom teaches believers how to live in the fullness of the Kingdom of Heaven and not according to what the world says.

The Spirit of Revelation -

The Bible says the Spirit searches the mind of God. I imagine the Spirit of Revelation like a big crane machine going into the mind of God and grabbing the information He had planned for you to know. The Spirit drops it on you, and you "get it." It is kind of an "Aha!" moment. You may have read the same verse a hundred times, but this time it suddenly makes sense and blows your mind.

Spirit of Revelation

Spirit of Counsel

The Spirit of Counsel -

Imagine you knew the wisest person ever, and they followed you around giving you advice. That's like the Spirit of Counsel. This Spirit will reveal to you what God thinks you should do or say. Sometimes, Counsel will show you what not to do or say. Before you do anything, ask the Spirit of Counsel about it, and you will never be given bad advice!

Spirit of Might

The Spirit of Might -

This is the dynamite-explosion Spirit of power. This part of Holy Spirit empowers us to do signs, wonders, and miracles. The Spirit of Might glorifies God because it is obvious that you could never do those things by yourself. It's a good idea to make sure you sit with the Spirit of Counsel so you know what to do when the explosion comes.

The Spirit of Knowledge -

This is the Spirit that gives you the heads up on things. He may tell you that the lady in front of you needs healing in her knee because of an accident twenty years ago. When the Spirit of Knowledge tells you things, it makes people say, "How did you know that!?"

Spirit of Knowledge

The Spirit of the Fear of the Lord -

This is the part of Holy Spirit that helps keep you humble. He reminds you of how powerful God is and how little you are. It keeps you walking the straight and narrow out of respect for Father.

Fear of the Lord

Keep your eyes open throughout the Bible for hints of these expressions of Holy Spirit at work. Here's a hint: 2 Chronicles 16:9 goes well with Revelation 4 and 5.

Questions for Chapter Seven

Fill in the blanks.

1.   List the Seven Spirits of God_____

     _____ _____

     _____ _____

     _____ _____.

2.   Isaiah _____:_____ is one place where all seven spirits are listed.

3.   The Spirit of Might and _____ work especially well together.

4.   The Spirit of the _____ keeps us
     humble and on track.

5.   Revelation 4 refers to the Seven Spirits as _____.

Chapter Eight:
Spiritual Gifts

Most parents love to give their children gifts. Parents may not be perfect, but they usually love their kids, and they enjoy making their kids happy. How much more does our perfect Father love to give us awesome gifts? He's a great Daddy, and His heart is bent on giving us the best! The difference is that when He gives us gifts, they aren't just for us. God freely gives us the things of Heaven, but He expects us to share them and help others. But how can you help others if you don't even know what gifts you have?

Spiritual gifts exist in us even before we are saved because God created us to have them. That is why you see different types of talents in people who are lost. Unfortunately, these gifts are not redeemed, or brought back to the purpose for which God intended them. People who haven't given their lives to Jesus and even some saints do not truly understand why they have been given the abilities they have. Many of them live frustrated lives because they are not able to see the divine design for which they are made.

Imagine that you were born with a natural talent for playing the guitar, but you never picked one up. What a waste! You would have had a blast learning to play the guitar and performing for the enjoyment of others.

Suppose one day, someone handed you a guitar. You picked it up and strummed it a little. You may have taken to it very naturally, but you still would need to practice to get really good. There's a lot to learn about music and how to express yourself through music.

You would have a choice. Would you practice playing your guitar and develop your gift enough to share it, or would you just go on about your business and never use the wonderful gift you had? That's the decision every believer has to make as well.

Father designed you as an important part of a whole picture, and it is time to start fulfilling the mission He created just for you. He has given you gifts to help you, and now you must learn what they are and how to develop them. So, in a way, by teaching you how to at least recognize these spiritual gifts in yourself, I'm handing you the guitar.

Please understand that what I'm giving you here is a start. It's like the beginner's guitar lesson book. This will give you the basics of several types of spiritual gifts so you will at least understand what they are. If you want to learn more, there are tons of resources about every gift, and I urge you to get some and read them. Then, most importantly, go give 'em a shot! You'd be crazy to read music books all day and never pick up an instrument and play it! You'd be even crazier to learn about the gifts of Holy Spirit but never use them.

Romans 12:3-8: A List of Gifts

Prophecy
Forth telling - to speak a direct message from God
Speak truth clearly
Sees "black-and-white"
High value on moral behavior and thinking
Absence of compromise
Testimony of Jesus: What's He saying and doing? (I learned this from Misty Honnald at The International House of Prayer)

Serving
Motivated to meet primary needs
Greek word is "diakonioia," from which we get the word deacon
Deacon means "to attend as a servant"
Helping to meet spiritual needs as well as physical

Teaching
Motivated to teach others
Gifted to reveal truths from the Word of God
Likes to 'study'
Anointed to search out truth

Exhortation
Motivated to encourage
Likes to build up and cheer on
To call near, urge on, to console
Good people skills
Vision casters
Brings understanding

Giving
Called to give
Motivated primarily to meet financial needs
Anointing to gain wealth
Share what they have

Leading

Administration
Bring organization to situations and to the work of God
Strong leadership abilities
Take action

Mercy

Motivated to meet emotional needs
Compassionate
Encourage others by manifesting the love and care of God

Revelation Gifts - Gifts That Uncover Things

Word of Wisdom - supernatural wisdom given for a specific situation or understanding about the future. It is a revelation from God that directs you to action, given specific facts. "Dude, we should do it this way, and things will work out."

Word of Knowledge - supernatural knowledge about a person or situation that is not known through the natural senses. "Dude, did get that scar on your face when you fell off your bike when you were three?"

Discerning of Spirits - supernatural understanding as to whether the Holy Spirit, the human spirit, or a demonic spirit is at work in a situation. The Greek word means "to separate thoroughly." "Dude, there's just something about them I do not feel good about."

Speaking Gifts

Tongues - a message from the Lord that needs to be interpreted. "Dude, shaba boomba rheua tooka." This is like getting things in a digital language and transferring it into a cell phone call with a voice.

Interpretation of Tongues - interpretation of the gift of tongues which will bring edification, exhortation, encouragement to the body of Christ. "Dude, what I feel she said was, "The Lord says, continue on my children. I agree with the direction you have taken."
(Personal prayer language or tongues does not need interpretation, but rather it is your spirit praying to God. Jude 1:20; I Cor. 14:2, 4, 14, 15)

Prophecy - a message from the Lord to build up and encourage the body of Christ. "Dudes, I had a dream last night that the building we wanted is on 3rd street."

Power Gifts

Gift of Faith - supernatural faith for a situation. "Dude, arise from the dead, right now!"

Gifts of Healings - supernatural gifts of healings. "Dude, you're leg just totally grew an inch!"

Working of Miracles - supernatural creative power. "Dude, watch the sandwiches multiply so we can feed all these kids."

A Mantle - comes from moving in an anointing on a regular, consistent basis and a certain level is maintained. "Dude, everywhere I go people get healed!"

Holy Spirit Shows up to Prove He's Real

You may wonder why Holy Spirit does the things He does sometimes. I recommend you ask Him that personally, but for now, understand that all of His gifts are for the purpose of building the Kingdom and glorifying Jesus. Here are some Bible passages about Holy Spirit and how He works:

> "But you shall receive power when the Holy Spirit has come upon you, and you shall be my witnesses in Jerusalem, and in all Judea and Samaria, and to the end of the earth."   Acts 1:8 ESV

> "However, when He, the Spirit of truth, has come, He will guide you into all truth; for He will not speak on His own authority, but whatever He hears He will speak; and He will tell you things to come. He will glorify Me, for He will take of what is Mine and declare it to you. All things that the Father has are Mine. Therefore, I said that He will take of Mine and declare it to you."
> John 16: 13-15 ESV

"*Therefore I make known to you that no one speaking by the Spirit of God calls Jesus accursed, and no one can say that Jesus is Lord except by the Holy Spirit. There are diversities of gifts, but the same Spirit. There are differences of ministries, but the same Lord. And there are diversities of activities, but the same God who works all in all. But the manifestation of the Spirit is given to each one for the profit of all: For one is given the word of wisdom through the Spirit, to another the word of knowledge through the same Spirit, to another faith by the same Spirit, to another gifts of healings by the same Spirit, to another the working of miracles, to another prophecy, to another discerning of spirits, to another different kinds of tongues, to another the interpretation of tongues. But one and the same Spirit works all these things, distributing to each one individually as He wills.*"

I Cor.12: 3-11ESV

"*And my speech and my preaching were not with persuasive words of human wisdom, but in demonstration of the Spirit and of power, that your faith should not be in the wisdom of men but in the power of God.*"

1 Cor. 2: 4-5 ESV

Questions for Chapter Eight

1. Spiritual Gifts are mainly for yourself. T/F

2. List the gifts found in Romans 12:3-8

    _____ _____
    _____ _____
    _____ _____
    _____.

3. Revelation gifts are gifts that _____ things.

4. List the three main categories of gifts. _____ , Speaking gifts ,_____.

5. A _____ consists of moving in an anointing on a regular, consistent basis

Chapter Nine:
Five Fold Ministry

When you looked at the title of this chapter, did you immediately think it had something to do with laundry? Were you wondering, "Five fold? Is that something you're supposed to do to a towel?"

If you had no idea what "five fold ministry" meant, that's okay. I didn't either. This is yet another one of those things I had never heard about until my friends and Holy Spirit started teaching it to me.

Guess what? It was in my Bible the whole time! For reference, check out Ephesians 4. This chapter mentions five positions in the church (body of believers), so that's where we get the name, "five fold ministry." That name is not specifically in the Bible, but it's like a nickname many people use to describe it. Each of these positions represents an office, or place of leadership in the body of Christ. The offices mentioned are apostle, prophet, evangelist, teacher, and pastor. Jesus is the only one who is all of these.

Notice that this passage says these leaders are gifts of Christ to His body. The gifts listed in 1 Corinthians and the other places we looked at earlier are individual gifts, but the ones in this chapter are leadership gifts. God gives these gifts to certain people for the specific purpose of building up His family. It doesn't mean these people are more special or important; it just means they have a particular role in the family. In a family, a mother or father isn't more important than a child, but they do have responsibilities that come with having children. They raise the kids, provide structure and discipline, offer safety, and many other things that make them truly awesome people.

In the same way, the leaders in Father's earthly family have authority and are to encourage, guide, and lead the others as they mature with Holy Spirit. Like your parents are the government of your house, the apostle, prophet, evangelist, pastor, and teacher are the government of Heaven on Earth. Jesus is the head, and He is in Heaven. These five roles or offices are like His shoulders. In Isaiah 9:6, the Bible says the Head is in heaven, and the government is on His shoulders, His ministers on earth.

It was Father's plan from the beginning for all of us to walk with Him in perfect maturity and unity. Jesus gave these gifts and roles to bring us back to where we were originally supposed to be. The ultimate goal is for us to live just like Jesus did. If you're anything like me, you're going to need lots of help.

The apostle, prophet, evangelist, pastor, and teacher help us grow and mature in what the areas they are good at. For example, evangelists are really good at leading people into the Kingdom and getting people "saved." Evangelists lead people to Jesus and teach other believers to lead people to Jesus as well. There's a lot more to it than that, but that's the general idea.

These offices are like a hand. To see how it works, imagine a hand producing a movie.

Apostle

Apostle -
The apostle is like the thumb. It touches all the other fingers, which means it can act like each of the other fingers as needed. When you make a fist, all the other fingers go under the thumb, which shows the authority and

headship of the apostle. The apostle brings wholeness and support to the body of Christ. He or she is the first in order, and is like the writer of the movie script. Everyone else is carrying out what is written in the script.

Prophet -

The prophet is represented by the forefinger. Just as this finger points the way, prophets show the body where God is saying to go. Prophets also give warnings, instructions, and encouragement, just like a movie director.

Evangelist -

The evangelist is similar to the middle finger. Just like your middle finger, the evangelist goes out the furthest. Evangelists get people gathered into the kingdom. They are the movie trailers or commercials that get people to go see the movie.

Pastor -

     The pastor is like the ring finger. In the same way that wearing a ring on this finger shows someone is married, a pastor is said to be married to the flock. Pastors are like shepherds who keep Jesus' people taken care of. The pastor is like the body guard on the movie set.

Teacher -

      The teacher is symbolized by the little finger, but don't let that fool you. Teachers bring balance to the hand by guiding believers, removing error, and training them up. The teacher is like an editor working to remove mistakes and make the movie the smoothest and best it can be.

Saint (all believers) -

Saints are able to do a good job of each of the things above. You'll be better at some than others. Saints are like the actors and stars of the show!

As with all Kingdom things, we can't forget the most important person – Jesus. Jesus is like the producer of the movie. He's the one writing the paychecks, so He gets the final say in all things. The producer works closely with each of the offices to see the movie come together. He empowers each one to be the best he or she can be, and the job each person does should honor Him.

That's one little picture of the five fold ministry and the government of Jesus on the Earth. Just remember, it's all about becoming more like Him and bringing His Kingdom to this world. If every part works together in unity and submission to Holy Spirit, we're guaranteed to create a blockbuster!

Questions for Chapter Nine

1. The fivefold ministry is found in Ephesians 6. T/F

2. The _____ points the way.

3. The _____ is like a shepherd.

4. All believers in Jesus Christ are saints. T/F

5. Jesus was all of these offices/gifts in one. T/F

Chapter Ten:
Vision

Why is everything in this book even important? You have been rescued, provided for, healed, given peace, and given all sorts of supernatural gifts. So what?

Here's what: You have been chosen by the Almighty God of the universe to fulfill part of His plan. This is what you've been looking for all your life. Purpose. Vision. Mission.

It really isn't that complicated. Unless you line yourself up with God's plan for bringing you ultimate satisfaction, you will always know something isn't quite right in your life. When you agree to give Him all of yourself, He will give you a life like you never imagined.

Like I said in the introduction, I knew Jesus for a long time before I ever caught sight of the true plan for my life. There is more to it than praying, reading the Bible, and doing good things. We are called to run into the darkness, plunder Hell, and restore what was once lost. How do you do that? Easy. Just learn from Jesus and do what He did.

He was a man in love with His Father. He only did what His Father told Him or showed Him.

1.   He listened to the Father and chose twelve men to pour His life into. Sure, Jesus spoke to the thousands, but He spent most of His time with just twelve. Of the twelve, three of them got even more specific attention. If Jesus thought twelve was a good number for one person to concentrate on, so do I. So, talk to Father and ask Him to show you who to spend most of your time with.

2.   Jesus was very clear that these twelve were set apart to take what He gave to them and give it to others. He taught them by words and stories. He demonstrated how to do things. He gave them what the Spirit gave Him. He laid His hands on them and spiritually transferred anointing to them. It's important to get close to Jesus and give what He gives you to those around you.

3.   He gave his disciples missions and instructions on how to bring the Gospel of the Kingdom to cities and regions. He said to tell people the Kingdom was near, to heal the sick, cleanse the lepers, cast out demons, raise the dead, baptize people, and make disciples, which means teach them all you know and "do life" with them.

4.   The disciples obeyed what Jesus said. Listening to Jesus' Spirit, they fulfilled the small steps and big vision Father had for them.

I've learned that no matter where I go, there I am. By that I mean that I am not really that different just because I go somewhere. I usually end up leading someone to Jesus, casting out demons, and seeing people healed. Every day, everywhere I go, my mission is the same. All of the things in this book work in every situation. Whether I am buying groceries, teaching P.E., talking with my friends, or going on vacation, I do the same things. I extend the dominion of the King by listening to the King. I spend time in intimacy with Jesus and can't help but see it affect everywhere my foot lands. And there's no difference between you and me. Jesus told all of us to do the same things.

I pray you'll take what you've learned in this manual and make it "real." Our generation is bored because most of us don't know what we are supposed to be doing. Well, here it is. Give your entire life to this King and His Kingdom, and I guarantee you will never be bored.

Before, I didn't know what it was to be discipled by someone on purpose. Now I do. I pray in Jesus' name that you will be drawn to someone our Father has planned to continue where this writing ends. Ask Father to bring you someone to walk beside you and pour their life into yours. But please, dear reader, don't stop there. Ask Father to bring someone to you who needs to be poured into.

There is a plan for your life. It isn't up to you to make your own way and figure it all out by yourself. All you have to do is what already makes you tick, and do it for the glory of God. Be the "you" God is so excited about. You do not have to wait until you are grown up to walk in the authority and power Jesus bought for you with His life.

Jesus was about doing His Father's business from the moment He was conceived. Father doesn't limit you by your age! Go! Walk in the anointing and power of Jesus, the King of all kings. His perfect Spirit is within you for a purpose. There's no Junior Holy Spirit!

Questions for Chapter Ten

1. Jesus chose _____ good men.

2. You have been commanded to disciple others. T/F

3. If you follow someone's teachings you are their _____.

4. You will know God's plan for your life only when you are an adult. T/F

5. You have the same Holy Spirit who empowered Jesus. T/F

About the Author

Lauren Caldwell lives on a ranch in West Texas. She enjoys spending her time with her husband, Cliff, and their three children. Lauren serves in leadership at **The Garden Apostolic Training Center** in San Angelo, Texas. **The Garden** hosts a school of ministry for adults and children to train the saints to minister to the poor and homeless, young mothers, hurting women, and just about any facet of life the Kingdom of Heaven touches.

The Garden ministers to people from all over the world and would love to help you in any way it can. Please contact **The Garden** through the website Http://**www.thegardenstc.org** or email Lauren directly at **lauren@thegardenstc.org**.

Appendix
End of Chapter Question Answers

Questions for Chapter One

1. Sozo/Soteria includes 1) **forgiveness** of sins 2) **eternal** life with God 3) healing for body and **soul** 4) rescue from **evil** 5) protection 6) wholeness 7) **prosperity**.
2. We are made of three parts: 1)**body 2) soul 3) spirit**.
3. According to John 3:8 the reason the Son of God appeared was to **destroy the works of the devil**.
4. The Gospel of Salvation is like **entering** the gates of a ranch.
5. Doing the work or extending the ranch is like the Gospel of the **Kingdom**.

Questions for Chapter Two

1. **Blood** has the highest trade value for life.
2. **All** authority on Heaven and Earth was given to **Jesus** first, and then He gave it to **you**.
3. We do things Jesus did by the power of His Spirit **in** and **upon** you.
4. John baptized with water, and Jesus baptizes with **Holy Spirit and Fire** according to Mark 1:6
5. "**Christ in you** the hope of Glory…" Colossians 1:27

Questions for Chapter Three

1. Gifts of Holy Spirit are listed in 1 Corinthians **12**.
2. Healing is part of salvation. **T**/F
3. Father created people to live in sin, sickness and disease. T/**F**
4. A demon is never to blame when someone is sick. T/**F**
5. Two basic types of prayers in healing are **request** and **command**.

Questions for Chapter 4

1. 1."Are they not all ministering spirits, **sent to minister for those who will inherit salvation**."Hebrews 1:14
2. Rescue from evil or Deliverance is part of Sozo Salvation. **T**/F
3. The two major doors by which demons enter are: 1) Intrusion 2)

Legal Ground.

4. The five doors of legal ground are: 1)**Disobedience** 2) Unforgiveness 3) Emotional **Trauma** 4) Inner Vows and **Judgments** 5)**Curses**.

5. Jesus came to get rid of the Old Testament. T/**F**

Questions for Chapter Five

Fill in the blanks.

1. Enemy forts are made of **feelings** and thoughts.
2. Demon spirits are really just ways of thinking. T/**F**
3. You can sometimes identify Root Spirits by their **fruit**.
4. The Root Spirits listed in this chapter are all there are. T/**F**
5. List the Root Spirits and at least one fruit of its presence:

These are only the answers I provide, variations are certainly possible.

1.**Infirminty**: fruit- Cancer
2. Divination a) python b) Jezebel c) **Ahab**
3.Whoredom: **sexual sins**
4. **Fear**: nightmares
5. **Anti-Christ**: denies Holy Spirit and gifts
6. Jealousy: **anger**
7. Bondage: **addictions**
8.**Haughtiness**: pride
9. Error: **eating disorders**
10. Heaviness: **depression**
11. **Lying**: "you're ugly."
12. **Deaf** and Dumb: always having accidents
13.Perversity: **homosexuality**
14. Sleep/Stupor: **procrastination**

Questions for Chapter Six

1. In what chapter of the book of John does Jesus pray that we would know Him, be with Him, and know we are as loved by the Father as He is? **John 17.**
2. **Meditation** is another word for concentrating on something.
3. Name two ways you can know Jesus better. **Praying and Reading the Bible**
4. It is good to copy others to learn at first. **T**/F

5. **Oil** is symbolic of Holy Spirit.

Questions for Chapter Seven

Fill in the blanks.

1. List the Seven Spirits of God **Spirit of the Lord, Wisdom, Revelation, Knowledge, Counsel, Might** and **Fear of the Lord**.
2. Isaiah **11:2** is one place where all seven spirits are listed.
3. The Spirit of Might and **counsel** work especially well together.
4. The Spirit of the **Fear of the Lord** keeps us humble and on track.
5. Revelation 4 refers to the Seven Spirits as **the eyes of the Lord and lampstand**.

Questions for Chapter Eight
1. Spiritual Gifts are mainly for yourself. T/**F**
2. List the gifts found in Romans 12:3-8
   Prophecy, Serving, Teaching, Exhortation, Giving, Leading, Mercy
3. Revelation gifts are gifts that **uncover** things.
4. List the three main categories of gifts. **Revelation Gifts**, Speaking gifts, **Power Gifts**.
5. A **mantle** consists of moving in an anointing on a regular, consistent basis.

Questions for Chapter Nine

1. The fivefold ministry is found in Ephesians 6. T/**F**
2. The **prophet** points the way.
3. The **pastor** is like a shepherd.
4. All believers in Jesus Christ are saints. **T**/F
5. Jesus was all of these offices/gifts in one. **T**/F

Questions for Chapter Ten
1. Jesus chose **twelve** good men.
2. You have been commanded to disciple others. **T**/F
3. If you follow someone's teachings you are their **disciple**.
4. You will know God's plan for your life only when you are an adult. **T**/F
5. You have the same Holy Spirit who empowered Jesus. **T**/F

The Garden Apostolic Training Center is primarily a School of Ministry in San Angelo, Texas that fosters spiritual growth. The center provides training to equip believers in Jesus Christ for the work of the ministry and to be victorious in all areas of their lives through the supernatural empowerment of the Holy Spirit.
There are several ministries and companies that are partnered with The Garden or are a facet of the ministry. Below are the following ministries and companies.

THE GARDEN
An Apostolic Training Center

Transforming Lives Through Jesus Love

 THE GARDEN -- The Garden School of Ministry is a two year school that prepares Christians to minister as Jesus did and does.

 -- Company 68 is a ministry under The Garden seeking to see wounded women empowered to fulfill their destiny in God.

 --Providence is a ministry under The Garden targeting the homeless men, women, and childern in San Angelo's region.

 --Garden Publishing Company is a company that publishes, edits, and formats works for publication.

 -- M4 Initiative is The Garden school of ministry for kids to abide in the love of God, grow in intimacy with Jesus, and walk in the power of the Holy Spirit.

For more of this book or other Garden Publishing Company books use this Order Form.

Name:_____

Address of Buyer:_____
_____
_____

Email:_____   Phone:_____

Desired book: How Many * :

_____   _____
_____
_____

Send this Order Form to the following address, and we will contact you about your order and will be glad to assist you with aquiring our literature:

Garden Publishing Company LLC.
10403 U.S. Highway 87 N.
Sterling City, TX
             76951

*Discounts available on large orders.

For a complete list of our titles, visit us at
www.Gardenpublishingcompany.com